AF529317

COGNITIVE CORRELATES OF ACADEMIC ACHIEVEMENT IN PRIMARY SCHOOL CHILDREN

COGNITIVE CORRELATES OF ACADEMIC ACHIEVEMENT IN PRIMARY SCHOOL CHILDREN

Subrata Saha

ABHIJEET PUBLICATIONS
DELHI 110094

ABHIJEET PUBLICATIONS
2/46 Tukhmeerpur Extension
Delhi 110 094
Phone: 22960492, 65698474
e-mail: abhijeet_singh@vsnl.net
abhijeet_singh@indiatimes.com
abhijeetpublication@gmail.com

COGNITIVE CORRELATES OF ACADEMIC ACHIEVEMENT IN PRIMARY SCHOOL CHILDREN

First Published 2007
© S. Saha
ISBN 978-81-8988620-2

Price: Rs. 380/- (INR)

[All rights reserved. No part of this publication may be reproduced, copied, stored in a retrieval system, transmitted or used in any form or by any means, whether electronic, mechanical, photocopying, recording or otherwise, without the prior permission from the author or publisher, except for a brief quotations in critical articles or reviews.]

PRINTED IN INDIA

Published by J.K. Singh for Abhijeet Publications, Delhi 110094, Lasertypeset by Gaurav Graphics, Delhi and Printed at Himanshu

Preface

Future development of a nation largely depends on the best possible use of its intellectual resources. Primary education may be considered as starting point for this venture. The objective of primary education in developing countries is to produce literate and numerate population that can deal with problems encountered at home and at work. In India there is a need to identify and foster the abilities successfully contributing to the achievement of primary school children.

Different authors in different ways have suggested that intelligence, creativity and cognitive style are of much importance among the different cognitive abilities influencing academic achievement of school children. Intelligence, an important mental ability, is closely related to the success in academic achievement of school children. Creativity, commonly termed as divergent thinking ability in Guilford's terminology, is another intellectual ability that influences learners, success in academic sphere. A great deal of emphasis is currently placed on the study of creativity of school children for understanding and predicting many facets of their academic achievement. Cognitive style, another important ability of intellectual process, plays a vital role in learners' academic achievement as every learner employs specific style of perception characterized as field dependent or field dependent in his learning environment.

In this book the content is organized in a coherent manner in four chapters on the basis of research evidences for predicting academic achievement of primary school children from the study of their intelligence, creativity and cognitive style.

The author owes his deep and sincere gratitude to Prof. Pares Chandra Biswas whose profound knowledge in education has been a source of inspiration in this quest.

The author had the rare privilege of getting guidance and encouragement from Prof. E. Paul Torrance, Honourable Director, Georgia Studies of Creative Behaviour, USA at all stages of investigation.

Of course, without the cooperation and assistance of the Psychometry Unit and Computer and Statistical Service Centre of the Indian Statistical Institute, Kolkata, this work would not have been possible.

In preparing this book the author expresses his indebtedness to the authors whose works were consulted and cited in the Bibliography.

This endeavour will be rewarded if this book generates interest among researchers and readers administrators, policy makers, teachers and students.

Dr. S. Saha

Contents

1

Introduction

Primary Education and Development

Primary education lays the foundation of economic and social development of any country. It improves the productive capacity of societies and their political, economic and scientific institution. It also helps reduce poverty by mitigating its effect on population, health and nutrition. The evidences of research and experience demonstrate such developments as consequent of primary education. All the newly industrialized economics with dramatic growth in the past forty years, such as, Hong Kong, Israel, Japan, the Republic of Korea, and Singapore, achieved universal or all most universal primary enrolment by 1965. Psacharopoulos (1985) found very high social rates of return and estimated that the returns to completed primary education are 27 percent and the returns to secondary education are 15-27 per cent. Lockheed, Jamison, and

Lau (1980) summarized that four years of primary education increased the productivity of farmers 8.7 per cent overall and 10 percent in countries undergoing modernization (largely in Asia).Reducing child date rate and population growth rate, a part of any development programme, depends heavily on educating women (Cochrane, 1979).The education of women is closely related to child health, as measured by nutritional status. Elementary education improves hygiene and nutritional practices, which improve child and infant mortality. A social sequence or greater education is the adoption of more "modern" attitudes. The influence of primary school on the adoption of modern practices was greater than that of other factors, such as, home environment, urbanization, etc.

Though the developing countries have made tremendous strides in expanding primary reduction in the past decades and many countries have achieved universal primary enrolment, most developing countries are still a long way from achieving universal primary completion .With the populations growing faster than primary school enrolment, many countries will have to make a vigorous efforts to reduce illiteracy over the next ten or fifteen years. Several education systems are in danger not only of failing to make quantitative and qualitative progress, but of losing ground in primary education.

To overcome the short comings, the first priority of primary education should be to increase children's learning in school so that most of students master the curriculum and complete the primary cycle. Second, access to school must be provided for all school-age children.

In only few decades the prosperity and quality of

life of all nations will be determined by today's children and their ability to solve the problems that face them, their families, their communities and their countries. Education unlocks this ability and investment in children's learning is the most important contribution a nation can make to a better future. The current financial crisis to many countries places obstacles on the efficiency with which primary education is managed. The knowledge gleaned from different countries effort to increase their education system should be developed and disseminated.

Primary Education in India

The awareness of the importance of primary education to the country's economic and social development was reflected in the constitution of India. Article 45 of the Indian constitution directs that the state can endeavour to provide free and compulsory education for all children till they reach the age fourteen years within ten years of the adoption of the constitution on the 26th January, 1950.

In light with the constitutional commitment of the county to provide elementary education to all children, educational facilities have got tremendously expanded during the post independent period. This is particularly true of facilities at the primary education stage.

According to the fifth All-India Educational Survey (1992) conducted by N.C.E.R.T, nearly 95% of the population are served by a primary school within a walking distance of 1 km. In West Bengal about $3/5^{th}$ of habitations, covering 79.71% of the population, have the facilities of primary education within the habitations. The percentages of the habitations having these facilities within 1 km is 94.53%, which covers 97.38% of the populations. This expansion has definitely helped in making primary education more easily accessible to a larger section of the population.

With the initiatives like District Primary education Programme (DPEP) and Sarva Siksha Abhiyan (SSA), new primary schools were established since 1994, the year in which DPEP was initiated. The same is also partly true because of the SSA under which quite a number of new primary schools have been opened since 2001.According to Mehta (2004), of the as many as 637469 primary schools opened up to 2004, 87.12% schools are located in the rural areas, more than half of the primary schools (53.12%) are located beyond 10 km from Block Head Quarters. In 2004, 70.62% primary schools are found with pucca building, 11.19% with partially pucca (permanent) building, 2.20% with kuccha (semi-permanent) building, 0.16% functioning in tents and 8.40% with multiple type (more than one type) building. Percentages of girls' enrolment in 2004 in rural and urban areas were 47.31% and 48.22% respectively. In 2004, average numbers of teachers per school in rural and urban areas were 2.56 and 4.47 respectively and pupil-teacher ratios were 44:1 and 40:1 respectively.

This large-scale expansion has resulted in the creation of educational facilities with widely varying quality in terms of institutional infrastructure, teaching-learning possesses as well as the quality of student passing out of these institutions.

Since achieving well-defined standards of learning by children in schools is a powerful indicator of success of the system that works, the National Policy of Education (N.P.E.), 1986 emphasized the need for laying down minimum levels of learning for each stage of school education as a prerequisite for setting performance goals.

The minimum level of learning that all children must achieve at a given stage of education is seen as one of the important prerequisite for infusing a sense of direction to the system and thereby paving the way for improving its accountability. Laying down minimum levels of learning may be viewed as a move towards greater relevance and functionality in primary education. One of the implications of this exercise is ensuring the acquisition of basic competencies and skills to such a level where they are sustainable and would not easily allow for relapse into illiteracy. Two basic considerations, according to Dave (1991), should be kept in view in this context. 1. The cognitive abilities of the children at different classes or grades corresponding to different stages of development and 2. The empirical reality in terms of the enabling conditions that characterized the primary education programmes.

The N.P.E. (1986) recognised that "a human being is a positive asset and a precious national resource which need to be cherished, nurtured and developed within tenderness and care, coupled with dynamism". Each individual's growth, according to the 'policy' (1986), presents a different range of problems and requirements at every stage-from the womb to the tomb. It implies that an individual individuality and dignity should be respected and his needs, interest, aptitude and abilities taken into account by educational system.

Thus the present system of primary education in India is determined to educate the coming generation that will have the competency to tackle its problems creatively with confidence and determination and with a commitment to human values and to social justice.

Cognitive Competencies as Goal of Primary Education:

Education affects development through its enduring impact on various dimensions of cognitive competence: literacy (reading and writing), numeracy, modernity and problem solving (Scribner and Cole, 1981). All countries try to update their education system by changing them with developing the skills needed to solve the problems of the future. As advanced education and training rest on the solid foundation of good primary education, development and inculcation of different dimensions of cognitive competency must be initiated with due importance at this stage. The cognitive competencies targeted by the primary curriculum of most of the countries mainly include basic and higher order literacy and numeracy.

Basic literacy requires several types of skills, which some believe, are ordered in stages that range from pre-reading to decoding to fluency (Chall, 1983). Pre-reading includes understanding the nature and function of print, reading common signs and labels, recognizing letters and some sounds (in alphabetic systems), and writing one's name. Decoding involves understanding the correspondence between letters and sounds identifying about 1000 common words, and reading simple texts. Fluency involves integrating pre-reading and decoding knowledge and skills, a recognizing about 3000 familiar words and derivatives, relying on context and meaning as well as decoding to identify new words, and reading more fluently.

The second cognitive competency is basic numeracy. Dossey and others (1988) define basic numeracy as a "considerable understanding of two digit numbers and their addition and subtraction, some understanding of multiplication and division, knowledge of relation of coins, and the ability to read information from charts and graphs and use simple measurement instruments.

But basic literacy and numeracy are insufficient foundation for further learning, which requires the ability to apply basic skills to new and more complex problems, that is, higher-order literacy and numeracy (or problem solving skills).

Higher order literacy implies that reading is a tool for learning new information, ideas, attitudes and values; the text goes beyond and language and knowledge that the reader has acquired through listening and direct experience. Many educators believe that children at all levels of basic literacy engage in higher order thinking when they are required to understand and interpret what they read.

Higher order numeracy is the ability to use basic operations to solve simple problems. One definition of proficiency in mathematics is that learners at the beginning of problem-solving level a) have an initial understanding of the 4 basic operations, b) can add and subtract whole numbers in one-step word problems and money situations, c) can multiply a 2 digit and a 1 digit number, d) can conquered information from graphs and charts and e) are beginning to analyze simple logical relations.

It means that at all stages of primary education students must relate to what is being learned and connect it with their own experience. The more that students connect with the learning material, the more rapid their progress will be in building a strong foundation on which the later stages of education must rest.

Conceptual Background of the Study

The future development of the world and of individual nations hinges more than ever on the capacity of individuals and countries to acquire, adapt and advance knowledge. This capacity depends, in turn, on the extent to which the population has attained literacy, numeracy, communications, and problem-solving skills.

Modern public education developed from two distinct educational traditions, one concerned with educating the elite and one with educating the masses. The objective of elite systems of education, according to Lauren Resnick (1987), has been to train intellectual elite, drawn largely from privileged social strata, in capabilities of reasoning, rhetoric, mathematical and scientific thought and other skills that today carry the higher order (thinking) label. In contrast, virtually all mass education systems have been established with the aim of producing minimal levels of competence in the general population. Mass education is, from its inception, concerned with inculcating routine abilities: simple computation, reading predictable texts, reciting religious or civic codes. Primary education usually takes the charge of developing such skills among the population of the country.

The official primary school cycle in most of the countries spans from four to six years, which is ample time for students to meet the curriculum objectives. For all countries virtually these objectives include developing cognitive competence, which encompasses both basic literacy and numeracy and the ability to apply basic skills to new problems. All countries, according to Benavot and Kamens (1989) not only incorporate the same subjects into the curriculum of the primary schools but give them the same emphasis. These subjects include language arts (reading and writing), mathematics, science, social studies and moral and aesthetic education. More than 50 % of the available time is spent teaching language skills and mathematics. Other areas receive relatively less attention. This consistency in emphasis was found remarkably similar worldwide, regardless of the level of economic or educational development of the countries, furthermore it was held steady since 1960s. This emphasis reflects the common objective of primary education: to impart basic as well as higher-order literacy and numeracy skills. Developing basic and higher-order thinking skills in primary schools for the masses is, thus, a new idea.

Although it is not new to include thinking, problem solving and reasoning in some one's curriculum, it is new to include it in everyone's curriculum. It is new to take seriously the aspirations of making thinking and problem solving a regular part of a school programme for all of the population (Resnick, 1987). Learner's competency in basic as well as in higher order literacy and numeracy is reflected as learning outcome in the academic achievement in respective subject. Bloom (1982) asserts that learning in individual task influences results on larger academic measures. Thus, success in student's achievement in school subject is a result of the mastery of skills targeted in the curriculum of primary education. This success in achievement is not always caused by the schools but may due to be the cognitive abilities of the students admitted to such schools (Jimenez, Lockheed and Paqueo, 1991). Individuals, according to Psacharopoulos (1975), with more ability are likely to obtain more education than those with less ability.

These observations allow the researcher to analyze the more discrete cognitive abilities and then compare their individual impact on the academic achievement of primary school children in specific subjects of school curriculum such as mathematics and language.

The underlying psychological functioning behind academic achievement of learners, according to Bloom (1964), involves perception and analysis of problem, searching for familiar element to guide action, restructuring of problem, classification of the problem as familiar in type, selection of abstraction (theory, principle, idea, method, etc.) suitable to the problem, use of abstraction to solve the problem and finally yielding solution to the problem.

This point of view was implicit in the suggestion by Bruner (1963). He argued that the major kind of intellectual behaviour consists in reorganizing data input from the external world, in such a way as to reduce the 'cognitive strain' of information processing. A new datum is rendered meaningful by being connected with past data which it resembles. This process of connection is called 'coding', and a set of related data is called a 'category'. The combinations (coding) of data are fur from random. They are, in fact, informed by the Coder's previous experience, they are not blind stabs, but effective in sights based on knowledge of the subject matter involved and of the relevant rules of the game. This means that a given event will tend to be coded in a similar way by most members of a given culture- coding becomes highly stereotyped and in fact 'convergent' in nature. Now the less, some people, despite their common cultural background retain the capacity to make novel and unusual coding which manifest themselves as divergent (commonly known as creative) thinking. Bruner has stressed the importance of convergent thinking (conventional intelligence) in the effecting of divergent breakthrough. Creative thinking seems to arise out of thorough familiarity with the field. Pribram (1964) has emphasized this point of view by arguing that original productions do not arise by chance, but they represent an extension of the already known. He emphasizes strongly that creativity arises out of conventional intelligence- the 'work' involved in thinking divergently is concerned with extending the boundaries of the conventional, and in widening existing structures. Creative functioning occurs when the boundaries of the known are first mastered, through convergent processes, and then extended, by the application of divergent process.

Related to the view that creativity interacts with intelligence in producing high level of academic achievement by building on the more convergent kinds of processes as a base, is the notion that there may well be an I.Q. threshold below which divergent processes can not operate, and above which they become independent McClelland (1958) and Anderson (1960) hold that divergent processes would only come powerfully into play if convergent processes had sufficiently developed to permit appropriate mastery of the relevant field. Torrance (1962) proposes about 120 as the I.Q. threshold beyond which creativity bears a relationship to classroom performance which is independent of I.Q.

Thus, creativity adds to achievement by building on to conventional intelligence and they are not independent intellective modes which operate separately from each other, but interdependent facets of intellect, although the degree of interdependence decreases as I.Q. increases.

Besides these cognitive abilities viz. intelligence and creativity, academic achievement seems to depend on the cognitive style through which information are taken in by the learners. Different learners go about the matter of getting data from their learning environment in differing ways, so that, for example, some pupils concentrate closely on a small portion of what is available for input while others attend, in a less punctilious way, to a wider sweep of information. The characteristic way in which an individual goes about taking information from the external environment is referred to as cognitive style. Most cognitive styles have in common property that they involve a dichotomy between, on the other hand, taking the world in large lumps and on the other hand, selectively attending only to chosen portions of the environment. The dichotomy can be restated as being a matter of paying attention to as wide a range of environmental properties as possible or selecting a few attributes to the environment and concentrating on processing them. The later strategy has the advantage that one can select a few highly task related and task-relevant pieces of information and focus attention to them. This makes for ease of coding and necessitates little accommodation (modifying of codes). In other words the highly selective kind of cognitive styles lead to overcome an embedding context. This ability, when develop, makes possible and analytical way of experiencing (Witkin, 1977).

On the other hand, taking in as much information as possible involves the risk of cognitive strain, necessitates frequent modification of existing categories, and makes intellectual functioning a more arduous tasks. It involves the advantage of being able to relate widely different looking data due to least censoring of the information available in the external world (Cropley, 1967).

Research observation delineates intimate relationship between dimensions of cognitive style and variety of performance measures and problem solving (Mc. Kinney, 1975; Ault *et al.*, 1972; Drake, 1970). The problem solving behaviour requires a thorough grasp of the deductive process, full awareness of relevant attributes of the essential concepts and needs for maximum information. The non-analytic child is deficient in using the deductive process and fails to select relevant attributes and information necessary for the solution to the problems. The characteristics of simultaneous scanning, deductive processing, recognizing relevant attributes and seeking maximum information are needed for success in academic achievement.

But in solving problems of achievement tests students are frequently required to "shift to strategies more suitable for the task in hand than their preferred strategy" (Witkin et al., 1967). It indicates that both analytic and global dimension of cognitive style are useful for solving different learning tasks.

In the light of the above discussion it is evident that cognitive abilities of the learners are the important correlates of their academic achievement.

Review of Related Literature

The researcher went through different literature, reports, reviews, research journals and periodicals with regard to the academic achievement of students and other cognitive abilities such as creative thinking abilities general intelligence cognitive style etc. Some of the important researches carried out in these areas have been presented below in the synoptic way.

Torrance (1959) reported the coefficients of correlation between divergent thinking and academic achievement ranging from 0.37 to 0.53 with a sample of seventy five children ranging from 4 to grade 6 in their educational level. When the effect of IQ was removed the subsequent partial correlations were still large as 0.23 to 0.48.

Getzel and Jackson (1962) focused attention on the relationship between creativity and academic achievement. They found no difference in academic achievement between high creativity group and high intelligent group-despite a mean difference of about 23 points in IQ between the two kinds of group.

Cline, Richards and Needham (1963) demonstrated that scores on creativity tests correlated significantly with high school science marks.

Yamamoto (1964) also compared the academic performance of secondary school children. His results showed that the divergent thinking group did as well on the Iowa tests of educational development as did the high IQ group, despite IQ difference of twenty points.

Joseph (1966) found that achievement test scores correlated significantly with divergent thinking and evaluative abilities.

Cropley (1967) investigated the extent to which creativity scores are related to school achievement in a study based on 320 Canadian children. The correlation coefficients obtained ranged from 0.16 to 0.42 when all children were considered regardless of their grouping on the joint IQ-creativity basis.

Kanderian (1970) conducted a study to find the relationship between school achievement and measures of intelligence and creativity for learners in Iraq. The study indicated that three of the Guilford test of creativity as achievement or with other variable. The fourth test

(test of fluency) showed high correlation with school achievement.

Counts (1972) obtained a high correlation coefficient between creativity and academic grade point average. His finding was that creativity and achievement was positively correlated.

Bracht and Hopkins (1972) in their longitudinal studies that there is a substantial relationship between the achievement difference among students who are encouraged to identify and develop individual learning styles and those who are not. The same achievement differences between the two groups may also be found several years later. They concluded that students who are not encouraged develop individual learning style achieve less than those who are encouraged through a system of identification and reinforcement.

Passi (1972) in an exploratory study of creativity and its relationship with intelligence and achievement in school subjects at higher secondary stage found that:

(i) the product moment coefficients between creativity on the one hand and nonverbal and verbal intelligence on the other were 0.266 and 0.335 (significant at 0.01 level) respectively,

(ii) girls were superior to boys in nonverbal creativity and boys were superior to girls in verbal creativity and

(iii) intelligence and verbal creativity although have low multiple correlation with achievement, contributed significant variance.

Ruth (1976) found that the correlation between creativity and achievement was statistically significant but very low.

Witkin, Moore, Goodenough and Cox (1977) observed that field dependent children do not well at solving problems in which essential elements must be isolated from a particular context and recombined into a new relationship. They concluded that there is a tendency to function in a more or less analytical fashion that characterizes an individual's intellectual activity.

Sharma (1977) in his study with 400 sample (200 boys and 200 girls) drawn randomly from uniform types of school found that (i) males were superior in creativity to females, (ii) high and low creative males were significantly differentiated on intelligence scholastic achievement, risk taking tendency, anxiety, home healthy and emctional adjustment scores, (iii) high creative males were high in intelligence and scholastic achievement but low in risk taking, (iv) high creative females were significantly high in intelligence and scholastic achievement than low creative females.

Mehdi (1977) undertook a co relational study on creativity, intelligence and academic achievement of 459 students ranging from VII to grade VIII in their educational level. The findings of the study were:

(i) creativity was slightly negatively related to intelligence in urban sample whereas it was positively related with respect to the rural sample, and

(ii) there was a significant relationship between creativity and academic achievement.

Singh, Mathur and Saxena (1977) studied creativity as related to intelligence, achievement and security-insecurity of secondary school students. The findings of the study were: (i) creativity correlated significantly and positively with intelligence (r=0.92), (ii) creativity and academic achievement of the students was significantly and positively related (r=0.506), and (iii) high and low creative students differed significantly with respect to security-insecurity trait.

Acharyulu (1978) undertook a study on relationship among creative thinking, intelligence and scholastic achievement. A random sample of 400 urban pupils (200 boys and 200 girls) was drawn from a dozen of schools located in Guntur and west Godavari districts of Andhra Pradesh. The main finding were : (1) there were no sex differences in intelligence, figural creativity and academic achievement in Telegu language, general science and social studies; significant sex difference in verbal creativity and achievement in English and mathematics were found in favour of girls; the performance of either sex was better on the verbal than on the figural TTCT, (2) the average correlation between intelligence and verbal TTCT (r=0.21) was not only significant but was also higher than that between intelligence and figural TTCT (r=0.10); these correlations were higher for girls then for boys. Further the correlations between verbal TTCT and school achievement were as high as those between intelligence and school achievement.

Gupta (1979) in his study with a sample of 100 students of class VII and VIII found that (i) there was a significantly positively relationship between creativity and intelligence (r=0.39), (ii) the creativity and academic achievement scores of the students were positively and significantly related (r=0.70), (iii) the students of high intelligence and high academic achievement scored significantly higher than the students of low intelligence and low academic achievement in creativity.

Jarial (1981) reported the following results in a study with 200 students of class IX. The findings of the study were as follows: (i) A positively significant relationship was found between the verbal and nonverbal creativity and intelligence of the students, (ii) Academic achievement was positively and significantly related to verbal and nonverbal creativity scores of the students, (iii) The arts students scores significantly higher than the science students and females scores significantly higher than males on verbal as well as on nonverbal creativity tests.

Onyejiaku (1982) in the study on Cognitive Styles, Instructional Strategies, and Academic Performance found that analytic boys in the expository group scored significantly higher than nonanalytic students. The analyses revealed no significant main effect of teaching methods. In no instance was a significant difference found for girls in respect to cognitive styles or teaching methods.

Gayatri (1983) studied the educational orientations and related factors effecting the academic achievement of university students. Major findings of the study were: *(i)* The cognitive style variation of studies did not lead to any significant variations in perceptions of environment, *(ii)* Students with field dependent cognitive style were found to express a definite preparatory orientation with an expressed need for continual feedback, structured course work and organized activity, *(iii)* Students with field independent cognitive style endorsed and exploratory orientation, preferring to work independently and with less structure in their environment.

Mainka (1983) under took a study on acquisition of concept in mathematics of pupils of primary school level and its relation to some personal and environmental variables of the pupils. The study revealed that (i) the majority of pupils who were promoted to the next grade did not show acquisition of concepts of the lower grade, (ii) a pupil did not acquire any concept to its fullest form in one grade but growth of mathematical concept took place at all levels with different degrees of individual differences, (iii) with increasing age, a pupil made up in one or other concepts in mathematics but his success in one concept was limited by success in other concept, (iv) The highest variability in the acquisition of mathematical concept was observed with pupils of grade III at primary school level, (v) mathematical concept developed better with pupils good in language and did not develop to their fullest form with poor with language, (vi) there at primary school level.

Dey (1984) studied the relationship of creativity to intelligence and academic achievement of national rural talent (NRT) scholarship awardees of high schools of three districts of Orissa. The major findings were: (i) there was a positive and statistically significant correlation between creativity and intelligence of the NRTS holders, (ii) creativity was found to relate itself to the subsequent total school achievement of the NRTS holders and (iii) intelligence of the NRTS awardees was correlated with their aweard selection test performance and total school achievement of the highly intelligent awardees was better that that of the highly creative scholars.

Nagose (1984) in a study with 429 junior college students observed that (i) high scholastic achievement in science was more dependent on high intellective abilities, (ii) divergent thinking abilities added substantially to better scholastic achievement in arts and commerce, (iii) numerical ability and inductive reasoning were important determinants among intellective abilities for high scholastic achievement in the science stream, (iv) Verbal ability and deductive reasoning were important determinants among intellective abilities for high scholastic achievement in the science stream, (v) divergent thinking ability (composite) was significantly related to scholastic achievement irrespective of academic stream, (vi) originality was an important determinant among divergent thinking abilities of high scholastic achievement in science and arts streams, (vii) flexibility was an important determinant among divergent thinking abilities of high scholastic achievement in the commerce stream.

Rajput (1984) studied academic achievement of 435 students of grade v in mathematics in relation to their intelligence, achievement motivation and socio-economic status. Major findings of the study revealed that (i) intelligence affected the achievement of studies in mathematics; there was superiority of the high intelligent group of students over average and low intelligent groups of students in their achievement in mathematics. Further, the average intelligent group was better achiever in mathematics than the other low intelligent group. (ii) in natural classroom conditions, the achievement of students in mathematics was not affected by their achievement motivation and (iii) the socio- economic status of the children affected the achievement of students in mathematics.

Dixit (1985) in a comparative study of intelligence and academic achievement of adolescent boys and gills studying in class IX and X obtained the following findings: (i) Among class XI students there was no difference in the academic achievement of intellectually superior and intellectually very superior boys and girls. (ii) At all other intellectual levels the academic achievement of the girls was superior to that of the boys. (iii) Among class XI students there was no difference in the academic achievement of intellectually superior boys and girls, (iv) At all other intellectual levels the academic achievement of the girls was superior to that of the boys, (v) In general the intelligence test scores the boys were higher than those for the girls, (vi) In case of the boys there was very high correlation between intelligence test scores and academic achievement and (vii) In case of the girls there was an average correlation between intelligence test scores and academic achievement.

Roach (1985) assessed the effects of field dependence, conceptual style preference, intelligence and sex on the reading achievement of 418 7th graders (mean age 11.58 years) in Jamaica, West Indies. Result showed that although they were related cognitive styles, field independence and analytic conceptual preference were not strongly associated. Results further showed the reading achievement had significant correlations with field independence, analytic conceptual style, intelligence, and gender and that females demonstrated higher achievement. When intelligence was factored out, the relation between reading achievement and cognitive style become nonsignificant, indicating that field independence is not district from general intelligence and specific abilities.

Testu (1985) investigated the relationship between cognitive style (field dependence-independence) and intelligence and the effects of cognitive style on performance of verbal and nonverbal tasks among 80 school children (42 boys, 38 girls, mean age 11 years). Results demonstrated that a strong positive correlation between field independence scores and IQs. In addition, field independent students performed better than did field dependent students on the visual -spatial and mathematics tasks. There were no significant difference between field dependent students and field independent students with regard to performance on the conjugation exercise. Result suggested that there was an interaction between and cognitive style and that this interaction influenced performance.

De (1985) investigated into the cognitive style and cognitive ability of tribal and notribal school pupils of the age group 12 to 14 years. Major findings were: (i) Tribals were more oriented towards field dependence and towards field independence than the nontribals, (ii) Male and female tribal and nontribal students differed to field dependence whereas this difference was not noticed in the case of field independence, (iii) The tribal and nontribal students did not differ among themselves with respect to the trait of creative thinking and similar results were obtained with respect to the trait of intelligence. A highly significant association among the three variables in case of both tribal and nontribal students was found and (v) cognitive style was found to be associated with academic achievement.

Chadha (1985) conducted a study a 48 undergraduates (aged 18-20 years) and arrived at the conclusion that low creative were significantly more field-dependent than high creative and that females were generally more field-dependent.

Singh (1986) examined some possible contributing factors to high and low achievement in Mathematics of 370 students of class XI in the stage of Orissa. One of the major findings of the study was that achievement in mathematics was positively related with intelligence.

Rastogi (1987) investigated the difference in intellectual

level and creativity of 30 male and 30 female field-independent or field-dependent Indian adults. Creativity but not intelligence was associated with cognitive style: Sex and the interaction between sex and cognitive style did not significantly affect creativity or intelligence level.

Sinha, Trivedi, Gupta (1988) conducted a study of high and low achievers with special reference to their intelligence and family variables of 100 undergraduates. Findings showed that scholastic achievement was significantly related to intelligence, socio-economic status, sibling position and family size.

Esquivel (1988) investigated the correlations among nonverbal reasoning ability, creativity and academic achievement in 160 gifted minority children in grades 1-18. Correlations reflected limited relations among these variables, except for a significant positive value between creativity and reading achievement.

Antonak (1988) examined relationships between scores of intelligence test and achievement test at grades 2, 4 and 6 intelligence co-varied ineffective as predictors of achievement at a later grade. The best predictor of achievement at a later grade was achievement at an earlier in all cases.

Dave (1988) in his study on pupils achievement at the primary stage observed that (i) achievement of children in language was found to be excellent in class I, good in class II, better than minimum in class III and minimum in class IV, (ii) achievement of pupils in mathematics was found to be excellent in class I & II, good in class III and poor in class IV.

Sawyers and Canestaro (1989) examined the relationship between a battery of creativity measures and real world creativity as measured by a design laboratory project and final grade in an interior design course. Findings from 81 college students indicated that ideational fluency is a valid predictor of student achievement in an interior design course.

Kim and Michael (1995) conducted a study to ascertain for a sample of 193 eleventh grade Korean high school students (92 males and 101 females) the extent to which performances in selected measures of creativity was related to school achievement. Finding showed that measures of creativity translated from TTCT show little relationship to school performance. Korean high school females exhibited higher average levels of performance on creativity tests than their male counterparts.

Srivastava and Chandiramani (1995) examined the effect of cognitive style and family environment on scholastic achievement of a sample of 100 students (50 boys and 50 girls aged 14-15 years). Findings indicated that students from structured as well as independent families showed better performance than other children.

Bawa and Kaur (1995) studied the relationship of composite creativity and other achievement of 600 students drawn from higher secondary schools of Patiala district. Results revealed that (i) there was a strong association between scores on creativity and academic achievement for both male and female students, (ii) creativity and academic achievement in languages tend to be better correlated than creativity and achieving in social studies and general sciences and © originality and academic achievement tended to be more strongly associated than academic achievement and fluency and flexibility.

Padhi (1995) studied the influence of creativity on

academic performance of 636 class IX students. Findings revealed that creative abilities were positively and significantly associated with different academic achievements and high creative were superior in achievement compared to low creative.

Cahan & Ganor (1995) in their study on Cognitive gender differences among Israeli children observed a continuous and considerable reduction in gender differences with respect to all cognitive areas among non-selective populations. Gender differences have virtually disappeared in the verbal realm, and they are slight for most spatial tasks, although boys continue to hold a clear advantage with respect to mental rotation. Even mathematical ability, long a province of males, has come to be relatively evenly distributed between boys and girls in non-selective elementary-school populations. Differences (in favor of boys) appear only in secondary school with respect to mathematical problem solving, and they are largest (about 0.5 SD) in the quantitative component of the Scholastic Aptitude Test (SAT).

Matsumoto, Fan and Chen (1997) in the study on Gender Differences in Mathematics Achievement found no gender differences when total-group means were compared. When the high end of math score distributions was examined, however, noteworthy gender differences favoring male students emerged. These differences became larger from the 8th grade to the 12th grade and were more prominent at more extreme score ranges. The observed gender differences for students at the high end of the mathematics score distributions are important because these students are likely to consider pursuing careers in science, mathematics, and engineering.

Leedy, Lalonde and Runk (2003) in their study on Gender Equity in Mathematics: Beliefs of Students,

Parents, and Teachers found that the traditional gender-based differences in the beliefs regarding mathematics persist even in these mathematically talented students. Furthermore, parents' responses to the questions regarding the role of mathematics revealed that mothers, more than fathers, focused on the computational aspects of mathematics, while fathers more than mothers mentioned the role of mathematics in science or as a language. Boys, fathers, and certain mathematics teachers admitted to a low level of gender stereotyping, as evidenced by their scores on the Mathematics as a Male Domain subscale. However, the girls, mothers, and mathematics coaches did not endorse this stereotyping.

All the studies cited above reflected the following major observations:

(i) Academic achievement and composite creativity are positively related with few exceptions where the relationships are relatively low or insignificantly negative. Among the different measures of creativity, the fluency and originality measures have positive significant relationships with academic achievement.

(ii) Academic achievement and intelligence are positively related with each other.

(iii) Academic achievement and cognitive style are related positively. Field independents show better achievement than field dependents.

(iv) Academic achievement depends on three cognitive factors such as creativity intelligence and cognitive style.

(v) The relationships between creativity and intelligence range from significantly positive to insignificantly negative.

(vi) Creativity and cognitive style are positively related. Field independents exhibit high creative thinking abilities in comparison to field dependents.

(vii) Intelligence and cognitive style are positively associated.

(viii) Gender differences on academic achievement, creativity intelligence and cognitive style indices are found in favour of both the sexes in different occasions.

(ix) With regard to the academic achievement in language and mathematics, the primary school children in India exhibit a trend of gradual deterioration in course of passing from grade one to grade four.

(x) Mathematical concepts at the primary stage of education are developed better with pupils good in language.

(xi) Most of the research studies are conducted with secondary school students. Researches with primary school children are very few in number in comparison to secondary and higher stages of education.

Statement of the Problem

A review of related literature and studies showed that the relationship of academic achievement (in different school subjects) with creativity, intelligence and cognitive style had not been definitely established with primary school children. It was realized that despite of different efforts, there remained much to be done with primary school children to reveal relationships of academic achievement (in different subjects) with the cognitive variables enumerated above. This gap in knowledge concerning the relationship stated above stimulated the researcher to explore the problem further. It can be conceived as shown in figure 1.

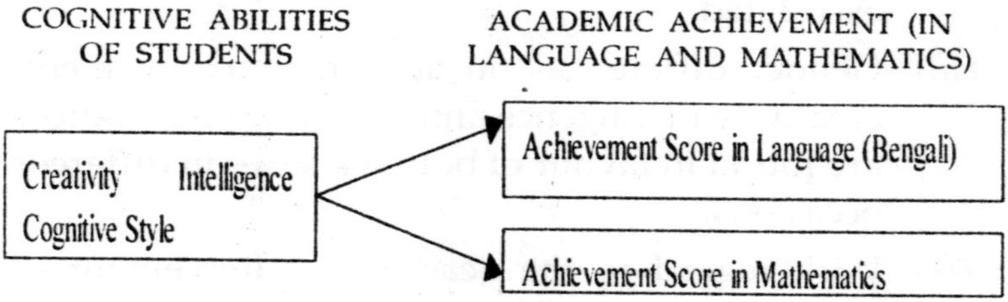

Fig. 1. Academic Achievement in Relation to Cognitive Abilities of Primary School Students.

But the researcher was aware of the fact that there might have some other variables (such as home climate, school climate, quality of teaching , curriculum, learning materials, learning time, socio-economic status etc.) which are also regarded as predictors of achievement. However, in the present study the researcher conceived the influences of these variables uniform for the sample to be drawn through the process of randomization.

The researchers decided, therefore, to investigate in to the relationship of academic achievement (the criterion variable) of primary school children with creativity, intelligence and cognitive style (the predictor variables) as well as to determine the potentialities of the predictor variables in predicting the criterion variables.

The problem was, thus, stated as

A Study on Relationship of Academic Achievement with Creativity, Intelligence and Cognitive Style of Primary School Children

Objectives of the Study

The following objectives were framed for the study:

1. To develop and standardize and academic achievement tests in Mathematics and Bengali(Vernacular) for class IV
2. To measure academic achievement in Mathematics and Bengali of the sample under consideration;
3. To measure creative thinking abilities, intelligence and cognitive style of the sample under consideration;
4. To find out gender difference, if any, on all the variables under consideration;
5. To make an appraisal of the extent of relationship among all the variables under consideration;
6. To develop a multiple regression equation of academic achievement in mathematics on creative thinking abilities, intelligence and cognitive style;
7. To develop a multiple regression equation of academic achievement in Bengali on creative thinking abilities, intelligence and cognitive style;
8. To find out the best predictor of academic achievement in mathematics;
9. To find out the best predictor of academic achievement in Bengali.

Delimitations of the Study

The study was delimited in the following way:

1. The sample of the study was delimited to include

only 505 students, both and girls, who were just going to complete the syllabus (prescribed by the Government of West Bengali) of class IV of primary schools situated at the urban areas in the district of 24-Pargaas (North) in West Bengal.

2. The content area academic achievement was delimited to include only Mathematics and Bengali (vernacular language) considering the greater emphasis usually placed on learning these two subjects in comparison to the other subjects of primary school curriculum.
3. The number of variables for the present study was delimited to include only 5 variables of cognitive domain. They were:
    a) Academic Achievement in Mathematics and Bengali as measured by the tests to be developed.
    b) Creative Thinking Abilities as defined by E. Paul Torrance.
    c) General intelligence as conceived by R. B. Cattell and
    d) Cognitive style as defined by Witkin and others.

Definition of the terms

• Academic Achievement

Academic Achievement means the quantity and quality of learning attained in a subject of study after a period of instruction. It means brightness in academic subjects. Academic achievements of school students usually encompass achievement in all the school subjects. But in this study academic achievement means knowledge, understanding and skills of application achieved by the students of class four in mathematics and Bengali (vernacular) only after following normal classroom instruction and prescribed syllabi in those subjects for a period of one calendar year. The indices of academic achievement are considered here as the composite score obtained by the students separately on the Academic Achievement Tests in Mathematics and Bengali.

- Creativity

In the present study the researcher conceived creativity as defined by E. Paul Torrance (1969). Torrance defined creativity as a process of becoming sensitive to problems, deficiencies, gaps in knowledge, missing elements, disharmonies and so on; identifying the difficulty, searching for solutions, making guesses a formulating hypothesis about the deficiencies, testing and retesting these hypothesis and possibly modifying and retesting them and finally communicating the results.

Operationally it may be defined as the abilities measured on the paper and pencil test used and expressed accordingly by the student scores on the creativity test. The different measures of creativity are proposed to be defined operationally in the following way:

a) Figural fluency

A score which shows the student's ability to produce number of ideas figurally.

b) Figural flexibility

A score which represents the student's ability to produce a variety of ideas figurally which may be classified into qualitatively different categories, e.g., to shift from one approach to another or employ different strategies, etc.

c) Figural originality

A score which indicates the ability of a student to produce unusual ideas figurally.

d) Figural Elaboration

A score which represents the students' ability to produce number of additional ideas figurally that contributes to the development of a general idea.

e) Verbal Fluency

A score that shows student's ability to produce number of ideas with words.

f) Verbal Flexibility

A score which represent the student's ability to produce a variety of different categories of ideas with words.

g) Verbal Originality

A score which indicates the ability of a student to produce unusual and rare ideas with words.

- Intelligence

Intelligence itself is a term with many meanings and reference. The definitions of intelligence are mainly functional in character. They state how intelligence operates through learning, adaptation, abstract thinking, etc. The nature of intelligence was conceptualized in varied ways which were far from uniformity. In the present study intelligence is conceived as the general mental ability, as defined by Cattell (1971), which is ubiquitous in its behavioural influence. Operationally, it consists in the ability to discover significant relation in a given situation or in the ability to educe relevant correlates or in a combination of these abilities. The index of intelligence of a particular student in the present study represents a score to be determined by the number of relationships perceived correctly from variety of given figural situations.

- *Cognitive Style*

Cognitive style is broad, systematic characteristics affecting an individual's perceptions to different situations. It means that cognitive style are characteristics, self consistent modes of functioning which individual show in their perceptional and intellectual activities.

Since cognition is a complex process comprised of many interrelated variables, the nature and importance of these variables are not always agreed upon with single interpretations by experts. In the present study the construct field dependence-independence is chosen as measures of cognitive style.

The person with field independence cognitive style tends to experience his surroundings analytically, with objects experienced as discrete from their background. The person with field dependent cognitive style tends to experience his surroundings in a relatively global fashion, passively conforming to the influence of the prevailing field or context.

Operationally the student's score on the test of cognitive style under consideration for the present study indicate the total number of the correctly found simple figures embedded within the complex figures. This provides a measure of the extent to which one's perception is influenced by the context in which an item occurs. Such scores form a continuous distribution. Accordingly, the designation 'field dependent' and 'field independent' like the designations 'tall' and 'short' are relative.

2

Procedure of the Study

Design of the Study

In the present study three important variables namely creativity, intelligence and cognitive style were included. All these important cognitive abilities play a critical role in the academic life of students. But the key problem in designing perfectly accurate study stems from a lack of adequate definition. It is not also possible to establish the discrete units of functioning within each of these specific skills. Moreover, there is no way to know exactly when one mental skill dominates another, or even, what combination of these skills is important to success in specific tasks, such as achievement in Mathematics, Bengali etc.

So descriptive research design was adopted to describe what existed with respect to the variables under consideration. The major aim was to determine the extent of relationship existing between criterions (academic achievement in Mathematics and Bengali) and predictors (creativity, intelligence and cognitive style).

The basic design proposed to study:

(i) the statistical significance of gender difference, if any, on all variables (both the criterions and the predictors) under consideration,

(ii) the extent of relationships existing among these variables on a sample of 4th grade primary school students gender wise if gender differences stood significant,

(iii) what actually does seem to influence the academic achievement in Mathematics and Bengali of 4th grade primary school students gender wise, if gender differences were significant.

Statistical Methodology

The researcher decided to follow the correlational method of descriptive research. This methodology helps to determine the extent of relationship existing between variables, that is, to ascertain the extent to which variations in one variable are associated with variations in another. The magnitude of the relationship is determined through the use of the coefficient of correlation.

Multiple regression is one of the most frequently used technique of analyzing data in behavioural research. Kerlinger and Pedhazur (1973) have defined multiple regression as a method of analysing the collective and separate contributions of two or more independent variables (predictor variables) to the variation of a dependent variable (criterion). It takes into consideration the co-variation between a set of independent variables with the dependent variable. One of the important aims of multiple regression analysis in correlational methodology is prediction. The objective of the present study is to know to what extent academic achievement can be predicted on the basis of variables like creativity intelligence and cognitive style. The researcher thus decided also to follow multiple regression analysis technique for the purpose of prediction.

Population of the Study

All the students of class IV of Bengali medium primary schools, following the Syllabus of Primary Education framed by the Government of West Bengal, in the district of 24-Parganas (North), West Bengal.

Sample and Sampling Technique

The sample consisting of five hundred five students who were just going to complete class IV of Bengali medium primary schools following the Syllabus of Primary Education framed by the Government of West Bengal, were selected from sixteen primary schools situated in the district of 24-Parganas (North), West Bengal. The total number of boys in the sample was three hundred eight and that of girls was one hundred ninety seven only. The process of sampling was as follows:

The researcher randomly selected sixteen primary schools from the list of available government and privately managed primary schools of urban locality in the district of 24-Parganas (North). As the sampling units were individual students, a pre-determined number of students were selected at random from the students of class IV of each of the sixteen primary schools to get the final sample.

Instruments

The researcher reviewed the different tests that could be used on the sample, particularly the 4th grade primary school students having Bengali as the medium of instruction, for the purpose of measuring creativity, intelligence, cognitive style and academic achievement of individual students. It was found that standardized tests of creativity, intelligence and cognitive style were readily available. But for measuring the academic achievement of 4th grade primary school students, following the syllabus of the Govt. of West Bengal, no suitable readily available tests were found. So it was become necessary to develop academic achievement tests in Mathematics and Bengali for measuring academic achievement.

Finally the following tools were identified.

(i) Academic Achievement Tests in Mathematics and Bengali to be developed and standardized by the researcher himself.

(ii) Torrance Tests of Creative Thinking, Form A (both verbal and Figural), developed by Torrance (1974) to measure the creativity of the sample.

(iii) Culture Fair Tests of Intelligence, Scale 2 (Form A and B), developed by Cattell et al. (1973) to measure the intelligence of the sample.

(iv) The Children's Embedded Figures Tests developed by Karp et al. (1973) to measure cognitive of the same.

Achievement Tests

The major function of achievement test is to measure students achievement and thus to contribute to the educational progress and attainments of the students.

It means that achievement tests are primarily designed to assess the knowledge, understanding and skills of examinee at a specific point in time. Achievement tests are thus tied to the narrow limits of those abilities which are established previously for a particular unit of school system. It means that achievement tests score should represent a se of components which can be objectively verified. A detailed analysis of educational objectives for students' achievement serves to broaden the test constructor's perspectives on what to test and how to test. In this context an outline of topics dealt with in instruction provides a useful basis for developing test items that will sample the desired achievement representatively.

The present researcher, thus, decided to construct objective based objective type test because in objective type tests there is often a good deal of more objectivity than in essay type tests. The student usually has more definite tasks, and the reasons for giving or withholding credit are more obvious to all concerned.

The most commonly used types of completely objective test items are multiple choice, true false, matching and classification. Among all these types the "multiple choice type, according to Ebel (1966), is widely adaptable and relatively high in ability to discriminate between better and poorer students ....Theoretically, and this has been verified in practice, a multiple-choice test with a given number of items can be expected to show as much reliability in its scores as a typical true-false test with almost twice that number of items". Considering such other advantages of multiple choice test over the other forms of objective tests, the researcher was convinced that objective based multiple choice test would become suitable for measuring the important learning outcomes of primary school children selected for the present study.

Construction of Academic Achievement Tests

Identification of Behavioural Objectives of the Academic Achievement Tests in Mathematics and Bengali:

Before constructing a valid test specific description of the subject matter to be tested was obtained. The different steps taken before the construction of the test items were as follows:

Construction of test items needs the realization of testable ideas and the expression of these ideas in the form of items. So the Syllabus (1979) prescribed by Directorate of Public Instruction (Primary Education) Government of West Bengal for Bengali (Vernacular) and Mathematics of class IV was thoroughly studied in order to analyse the content and emphasis placed on various aspects. The text books prepared by the Directorate of School Education (Primary Eduycation), Government of West Bengal for the students of class IV were carefully analysed in order to realize the minimum level of learning expected from the children. The text books published by National Council of Educational Research and Training (N.C.E.R.T.), New Delhi for the primary school children were also consulted to keep in touch with the objectives set by the Government of India for the education of primary school children of the country. Besides these the Report of the Committee (1991) set up by the Ministry of Human Resource Development (Department of Education), Government of India, for determining minimum levels of learning at primary stage, Inservice Teacher Education Package for Primary School Teachers (1988). Shikshan Dipika (Curriculum Guide) for Primary

Education of West Bengal (1986) was studied thoroughly for determining the objectives of tests to be constructed. In this context experts' opinion were collected from different Primary Teacher Educators of the State and also from the experienced Primary School Teachers. Thus relevant information became available for the preparation of test items.

On the basis of this analysis the following behavioural objectives were identified by the present researcher for constructing Academic Achievement Tests in Mathematics and Bengali.

Behavioural Objectives of Academic Achievement Test in Mathematics:

The learner will be able to:

(1) add the largest number of 5-digit with the smallest number of 4-digit.

(2) add proper fractions having same denominator.

(3) subtract a proper fraction from the other having same denominator.

(4) reduce a given fraction to lowest term.

(5) find the number of buses required for definite number of passengers when the passenger capacity of the bus is given.

(6) find the prime factors of a given number.

(7) fill in the blank (numerator) of simple arithmetical expression of equivalent fraction.

(8) find the product of all the even numbers given within a set of numbers.

(9) calculate the remainder of a division process when the divisor and dividend are given in the form of a problem.

(10) calculate the quantity of fluid contained in a given number of containers when the capacity of each container is supplied.

(11) fill in the blank of a simple arithmetical expression given in the form of multiplication.

(12) find the multiples of a given number from a given range of numbers.

(13) fill in the blank (denominator) of simple arithmetical expression of equivalent fraction.

(14) identify the geometric shape of a particular portion of a given picture.

(15) find the largest fraction from a given set of fractions.

(16) identify the geometric shape of the object in a given picture.

(17) solve the problem of calculating the total distance traveled by different means.

(18) solve problem involving three basic operations of multiplication, subtraction and division.

(19) form the largest possible number using all the given digits.

(20) count the number of rectangles and circles in a given complex figure.

(21) find out the largest number from the set of given numbers.

(22) convert different numbers of different paise into money to get the total amount when given in the form of a problem.

(23) find the lowest number needs to be added with the total of given set of numbers to make it an odd number.

(24) identify the odd number next to a given 4-digit number.

(25) calculate the price of given quantity of milk when the rate of price of milk for litre is given.

(26) find the maximum number of individuals among which different numbers of different fruits can be equally distributed.

(27) find the common multiples of two given numbers from a given range of numbers.

(28) multiply a decimal fraction by a single digit number.

(29) identify a particular geometric shape excluding other geometric shapes given in a complex figure.

(30) divide a 2-digit number by10 to yield a quotient of decimal fraction.

(31) calculate the maximum number of rows required to implant seedlings purchased in different numbers in two different occasions.

(32) solve the problem of finding the average age of persons of different ages.

(33) do simple division to yield a quotient of decimal fraction.

(34) multiply a decimal (of two places) fraction by 100.

(35) calculate the quantity of fluid remained in the vessel when a given quantity of fluid is poured into another vessel.

(36) find out the H C F of given numbers.

(37) find out the largest number by which two given numbers are completely divisible.

(38) solve the problem of calculating average price

of purchase when the price of different articles are given.

(39) find the length of the unused tape when its full length and the length of the portion used are given in the form of a problem.

(40) solve the problem to find the largest fraction from the given fractions of a unit.

(41) count the number of triangles in a given figure.

(42) solve the problem involving addition and subtraction of fractions.

(43) calculate the amount of money spent when the total amount of money and other expenditure made are given in the form of a problem.

(44) find the common factors of two given numbers.

(45) find the number of objects possessed by an individual when the number of objects possessed separately by the others and the average number of objects are given in the form of a problem.

(46) divide a decimal fraction by 100.

(47) solve simple problem on addition of fractions having different denominators.

(48) solve the problem of finding the balance in hand when the total amount of money and the cost of different articles are given.

(49) solve the simple problem on lcm.

(50) find the average of all even numbers given within a set of numbers.

(51) find the rate of income per day of an individual when the total amount of money earned in specific number of days are given.

(52) find the distance between two extreme poles when

the distances between the intermediary poles are given.

(53) find out the smallest number which is completely divisible by a set of given numbers.

(54) find the number of units when the average and sum total are given in the form of a problem.

(55) multiply a decimal (of two places) fraction by 100.

Behavioural Objectives of Academic Achievement Test in Bengali

The learner will be able to:

(1) find the suitable conjunction to fill in the blanks of the given sentence.

(2) find the adjective (say 'learned') to fill in the blank of the given sentence.

(3) find the word opposite in meaning to the given word (say 'weak').

(4) find the suitable verb to complete the given sentence (in present continuous tense).

(5) find the suitable pronoun (say 'he/she') to fill in the blank of the given sentence.

(6) complete the given sentence by selecting a suitable word which duplicates the relationship (say 'movement') implied in the sentence.

(7) identify the required information (say 'position of the head of pigeon') from the given text.

(8) complete the given sentence by selecting a suitable word which duplicates the relationship (say 'occupation') implied in the sentence.

(9) locate the required information (say 'the sleeping place of the cat') from the given text.

(10) find the adjective (say 'gentle') to fill in the blank of the given sentence.

(11) realize the main idea (say "a friend in need a friend in deed') of the given text.

(12) find the suitable verb (in relation to first person) to complete the given sentence.

(13) find the required information (say 'the nature of Ramu') from the given text.

(14) realize the main idea of the given rhyme.

(15) select suitable conjunction (say 'but') to complete the given sentence.

(16) indicate the meaning of the given word (say 'prestige').

(17) find the meaning of the given word (say 'shelter').

(18) select the suitable verb to complete the given sentence (in the past tense).

(19) supply the suitable verb (in relation to third person) to complete the given sentence.

(20) realize the main idea (say "nobody believes a liar') of the given text.

(21) locat the required information (say 'wheather forecast') from the given text.

(22) find the suitable pronoun (say 'we') to complete the given sentence.

(23) recognise the season (say "winter') from the description of different vegetables, foods etc. available during he season.

(24) establish the cause of an action (say 'deep tube-well plumbing') described in the given text.

(25) identify the required event (say 'dance') from the other events described sequentially in the given text.

(26) recognise the word opposite in meaning to the given word (say 'cruel').

(27) find the suitable verb t complete the given sentence (in the past tense).

(28) complete the given sentence with a suitable word which duplicates the relationship (say 'place of work') implied in the sentence.

(29) identify the pronoun (say 'your') to complete the given sentence.

(30) identify the pronoun 9say 'him/.her') to complete the given sentence.

(31) complete the given sentence with a suitable word which duplicates the relationship (say 'driver') implied in the sentence.

(32) split up a complex sentence into two simple sentences.

(33) locate the main idea (say "failures are the pillars of success') of the given text.

(34) join the two simple sentences (given) to forma complex sentence.

(35) find suitable conjunction (say 'and') to complete the given sentence.

(36) recognise the meaning of the given word (say 'fear').

(37) recognise the meaning of the given word (say 'cover').

(38) recognise meaning relationship between two different words given.

(39) find the adjective (say 'tall') to complete the given sentence.

(40) identify the required object (say 'wall') from the other objects described sequentially in the given text

(41) identify the pronoun (say 'them') to complete the given sentence.

(42) recognise meaning relationship between two different words given.

(43) recognise meaning relationship between two given synonymous words.

(44) find suitable verb to complete the given sentence (in the future tense).

(45) identify the meaning of the given word (say 'exhibition').

(46) recognise the meaning relationship between two given different words.

(47) find the antonym of a given word (say 'perplex').

(48) join the two simple sentences given.

(49) establish the cause of an event described in the given text.

(50) find the word opposite in meaning to the given word (say 'silent').

(51) recognise the meaning relationship between the two given synonymous word.

(52) identify the meaning of the given word (say 'excuse').

(53) recognise the meaning relationship between the two given words (say 'opposite in meaning').

(54) locate the required information (say 'about windows') from the given text.

(55) recognise the meaning relationship between the two given synonymous words.

(56) find the meaning of the given word (say 'fear'),

(57) find the antonym of the given word (say 'fast').

(58) complete the given sentence with a word which

duplicates the relationship (say 'respiration') implied in the sentence.

(59) join the two given sentence to form a complex sentence.

(60) recognise the meaning relationship between the two given words (say 'opposite in meaning').

Construction of Pre Try-out Forms of the Academic Achievement Tests in Mathematics and Bengali

The items of the tests were assembled into a pre-try out form. Out of a pool of 120 items in each of the two subjects like Mathematics and Bengali, the pre-try out test in each subject consisted of 88 items. The item pool (multiple choice type) was sent to few experts to judge the items. Subject specialists were also requested to arrange the items in a rough order of difficulty.

Determining Test Length

The decision abut the length of the test or the number of items to be included should be considered with due importance. It was realized that the proposed tests should be such as could be administered easily within the frame work of normal activities of the schools, i.e., without disrupting their normal functioning. Thus it was decided that each try-out form of the tests should have the duration of 60 minutes.

Construction of Try-out Forms of the Academic Achievement Tests in Mathematics and Bengali

On the basis of experts' opinion the pre-try out forms were scrutinized thoroughly and 23 items were further eliminated from each form. The total number of items thus selected for each of the try out forms was 65.

Try-out of the Academic Achievement Tests in Mathematics and Bengali

The try-out forms of the tests were administered on a representative sample of 300 students consisting of boys and girls of class IV of primary schools. The environmental and psychological conditions were kept normal at the time of administering the tests. The Academic Achievement Test of Bengali was administered first followed by the Academic Achievement Test in Mathematics with an interval of 10 minutes between the two administrations. The difficulties faced by the students were noted and attended to. A considerable time was allowed to the students to complete the answers. It was found that the average time taken by the students was 55 minutes.

Scoring Principles of the Academic Achievement Tests in Mathematics and Bengali

Both the tests of Mathematics and Bengali were comprised of multiple choice items with five or three distracters. To make the scoring easier, it was decided that the item attempted successfully would be credited with marks one ('1') and for unsuccessful attempt or omission zero ('0') marks would be given. The total score equals the number of items answered correctly.

Item Analysis of the Academic Achievement Tests in Mathematics and Bengali

The quality and merit of a test depend upon the individual items of which it is composed. The analysis of students' response to objective test items is a powerful tool for test improvement.

In evaluating items, two major aspects are considered:

the level of difficulty and the discriminative value of each item.

Difficulty Value

The difficulty of an item is defined in terms of percentage (or proportion) of persons who answer I correctly. The easier the item, the larger will this percentage be. There is no formula for determining the exact distribution of item difficulties. A common practice is to select some items whose difficulty is at, or close to, the 50 per cent level and other items with a wide range of degree of difficulty in terms of per cent passing. For the selection of items of the present tests the range of 10 per cent to 87 per cent difficulty value was accepted.

Discriminative Value

Item discrimination refers to the degree to which an item differentiates correctly among examinees in the behaviour that the test is designed to measure. There are numerous indices and procedures for determining discriminative value of an item.

In the present study discriminative indices of the items were determined on the basis of the relation of an item to the total score of its test. The total score on the test whose items were analyzed was used as the criterion rather than some other independent (external) measure of achievement.

The fact is that the score of an item being analyzed contributes to the total score on the test, the criterion against which the item is being tested. The selection of highly discriminating items, using total test score as the criterion, results in a test whose items are valid measures of what the whole test measures. In this sense, item analysis is a technique of item validation. Thus, the index of validity may mean how well the item measures or discriminates in agreement with the rest of the test.

After working out the difficulty and discriminative indices of 65 items in each try out form of both the tests, it was found that

(i) the discriminative indices of the items of Mathematics test were in the rage of .02 to .51 and the same for the items of Bengali test were in the range of .08 to .62.

(ii) the difficulty values of the items of Mathematics test were in the ranger of 9 to 82 per cent and the same for the items of Bengali test were in the rage of 18 to 87 per cent.

The frequency distributions of discriminative indices and difficulty values of the items in the try-out form and after items analysis for each test have been given in Tables 1-4.

Table 1: Discriminating Indices of Items in the Try-out and in the Final Form after Item Analysis of the Achievement Test in Mathematics

Discriminating value	*No. of items in the Try-out form*	*No. of items eliminated*	*No. of items retained*
.45 - .54	8	-	8
.35 - .44	25	-	25
.25 - .34	19	-	19
.15 - .24	7	4	3
Below .14	6	6	-
Total	65	10	55

Table 2: Discriminating Indices of Items in the Try-out and in the Final Form after Item Analysis of the Achievement Test in Bengali

Discriminating value	*No. of items in the Try-out form*	*No. of items eliminated*	*No. of items retained*
.55 - .64	8	-	8
.45 - .44	19	-	19
.35 - .34	22	-	22
.25 - .24	11	4	11
.15 - .24	3	3	
Below .14	2	2	-
Total	65	5	60

Table 3: Difficulty values of Items in the Try-out and in the Final Form after Item Analysis of the Achievement Test in Mathematics

Difficulty value	*No. of items in the Try-out form*	*No. of items eliminated*	*No. of items included in the final test*
80 – 89	1	-	1
70 – 79	-	-	-
60 – 69	-	-	-
50 – 59	7	-	7
40 – 49	9	1	8
30 - 39	7	-	7
20 – 29	12	1	11
10 – 19	24	4	20
0 - 9	5	4	1
Total	65	10	55

Table 4: Difficulty Values of Items in the Try-out and in the Final Form after Item Analysis of the Achievement Test in Bengali

Difficulty value	*No. of items in the Try-out form*	*No. of items eliminated*	*No. of items included in the final test*
80 – 89	4	-	4
70 – 79	14	-	14
60 – 69	9	-	9
50 – 59	3	-	3
40 – 49	11	1	10
30 - 39	13	2	11
20 – 29	10	2	8
10 – 19	1	-	1
0 - 9	-	-	-
Total	65	5	60

Selection of Items for the Final Forms of Academic Achievement Tests in Mathematics and Bengali

The discriminative indices of items in between .18 and .541 were chosen for final test in Mathematics and discriminative indices of items in between .26 and .62 were chosen for final test in Bengali. So out of 65 items in each try out form of both the tests, 10 items in Mathematics and 5 items in Bengali had to be dropped on technical ground.

Thus, the selected items (55 in Mathematics and 60 in Bengali) were then arranged in order of their difficulty values (from larger to smaller value of difficulty) to prepare the Final Tests in both the subjects.

- ***Administration of the Final Tests of Academic Achievement in Mathematics and Bengali***

The final forms of both the achievement tests in Mathematics and Bengali were administered on large sample of 505 students of class IV duly selected for the purpose. The sample includes boys and girls from the Bengali medium primary schools in the district of 24-Parganas (North).

The test of Bengali was administered first followed by the test of Mathematics. The first four periods in each school were taken for administration of both the tests with an interval of 10 minutes after the first administration.

- ***Determination of Reliability of the Academic Achievement Tests in Mathematics and Bengali***

After developing the final version of the achievement tests, it was become necessary to determine the reliability of the tests.

It was decided that two types of reliability coefficient (Cronbach Alpha for estimating internal consistency and test-retest for estimating stability) had to be computed for each of the two achievement tests.

Cronbach Reliability

The method fo: finding, reliability, utilizing a single administration of a single form, is based on the consistency of responses to all items in the test. This inter item consistency is usually estimated by using the following formula as proposed by L.J. Cronbach.

$$\alpha = (n/n\text{-}1) \times (1 - \Sigma Vi / Vt)$$

where, Vi = item variances

Vt = variance of total scores

n = number of items in a test

When the items of a test are scored either 1 or 0, this formula takes the form of usual Kuder-Richardson Formula 20 (K-R formula 20). The essential characteristic of this method is that the criterion is none other than the total score on the test itself.

The reliability co-efficient determined by Cronbach method has been shown in Table 5.

Table 5. Reliability Coefficients (∝) of Academic Achievement Tests

Method	*N*	*Reliability Coefficient*	
		Mathematics	***Bengali***
Cronbach Alpha	505	.90*	.93*

* P < .01

Test-retest Reliability:

In the present study retest was done after an interval of three weeks. The tests were read ministered on a sample of 300 students in the almost similar physical, psychological and environmental conditions as were during the first administration.The reliability coefficients determined by test retest method has shown in Table 6.

Table 6. Reliability Coefficients of Academic Achievement Tests

Method	*N*	*Reliability Coefficient*	
		Mathematics	***Bengali***
Test- Retest	300	.81*	.85*

* P < .01

- ***Determination of Validity of the Academic Achievement Tests in Mathematics and Bengali***

Since, according to Ebel (1966), "Criterion scores that measure exactly the same thing as the test is intended to measure are seldom available, even in more liable form, for most classroom tests of educational achievement, the best procedures for establishing the validities of tests of educational achievement are usually those involving direct validation".

This is true for the present study also. No exact and reliable criterions were available for validating the achievement tests of the present study. It was, thus, decided that the content validity and intrinsic validity of the tests would be the best measures of validity.

Content Validity:

Content validity involves essentially the systematic examination of the test content to determine whether it covers a representative sample of the behaviour domain to be measured. Taken collectively, the items of the test should constitute a representative sample of the variable to be tests. The following steps were taken to bring content validity in the development of achievement tests.

(i) Adequacy of Sampling of Content

In order to achieve this, the content areas of both the subjects, Mathematics and Bengali, were systematically analyzed to make certain that all major aspects were adequately covered by the test items and in the correct proportion.

(ii) Objective Based Test Items

In the development of achievement tests, items were

matched to the instructional objectives and the instructional objectives, were in turn, relevant to the content selected. Items of the tests were judged by a jury of experts. Necessary modification and omission of items were made as per the judgment of the experts. So it can be logically argued that the achievement tests have content validity.

(iii) Building the Test Blue-print

For ensuring content validity of the achievement tests specifications were set up in the form of test blue prints.

Intrinsic Validity

The degree to which a test measures what it measures may be called is intrinsic validity. This definition can also be stated in terms of how well the obtained scores measure the test's true score components. This validity is indicated by the square root of the proportion of true variance, in other words, the square root of its reliability as shown in the following equation.

$$r_t = \sqrt{r_{tt}}$$

Where, r_t = the correlation between obtained and true score,

r_{tt} = the reliability coefficient of the test.

It measures the independent ability of test scores by showing how well obtained scores agree with heir true values. The validity for the achievement tests thus determined has been given in Table 7.

Table 7. Validity from the Index of Reliability of Tests Scores

Sl.No.	Achievement test	r_{tt}	$r_t = \sqrt{r_{tt}}$
1.	Mathematics	0.81	0.90
2.	Bengali	0.85	0.92

Setting up the Norms for the Academic Achievement Tests in Mathematics and Bengali

The raw scores of the Academic Achievement Tests in Mathematics and Bengali were transformed into the T-scores. The T-score Norms for the Tests in Mathematics and Bengali have been shown in Tables 8 and 9.

Table 8. Norms of the Achievement Test in Mathematics

Scores	*T-score*	
	Boys	**Girls**
50 – 54	79	-
45 – 49	71	-
40 – 44	67	-
35 – 39	64	-
30 – 34	61	78
25 – 29	58	70
20 – 24	55	63
15 – 19	51	56
10 – 14	45	48
5 – 9	39	39
0 - 4	30	30

Table 9. Norms of the Achievement Test in Bengali

Scores	*T-score*	
	Boys	**Girls**
60 – 64	79	-
55 – 59	71	-
50 – 54	63	78
45 – 49	58	74
40 – 44	55	66
35 – 39	52	59
30 – 34	49	57
25 – 29	46	48
20 – 24	43	44
15 – 9	40	40
10 - 4	35	35
5-9	30	30
0 - 4	23	24

Description of Torrance Tests of Creative Thinking

Torrance Tests of Creative Thinking (TTCT) developed by Prof. E. Paul Torrance and published by Scholastic Testing Service, U.S.A. is a paper-and-pencil test consisting of four batteries namely Verbal Form A and Verbal Form B (an equivalent form of verbal form A) and Figural Form A and Figural Form B (an equivalent form of Figural Form A.). The verbal test battery of Torrance Test of Creative Thinking is labeled "Thinking Creatively with Words' and the figural test battery is labeled 'Thinking Creatively with pictures'. The tests are described as suitable from kindergarten to graduate school.

The Verbal Form A and Figural Form A of Torrance Tests of creative thinking were used for assessing creativity in the present study.

The scoring procedure used in the present investigation was the same as given in the TTCT direction manual and scoring guide. The verbal battery yields a total score in each of three traits: Fluency, flexibility and originality. From the figural battery four total scores are obtained in the traits of fluency, flexibility, originality and elaboration.

Description of Cattell's Culture Fair Tests of Intelligence, Scale 2

The Culture Fair Intelligence Test, developed by R.B. Cattell and published by the Institute for Personality and Ability Testing (IPAT), is a paper-and-pencil test. This test is available in three levels. Scale 1, for ages 4 to 9 and mentally retarded adults, scale 2, for ages 8 to 13 and average adults, and scale 3, for Grades 10 to 16 and superior adults. Each scale has been prepared in two parallel forms A and B.

In the present study "scale 2" (both the forms) was used for measuring intelligence because the average age of the sample was 9 + years. This scale is group administrable. Each form of scale 2 contains four subtests, involving different perceptual tasks so that composite intelligence measure avoids spurious reliance on a single skill.

The items are scored either 1 or 0. Since a correct answer is scored 1 and any other answer 0, the total score of an individual equals the number of items answered correctly, 46 being the maximum score in each form. In the present study the average of the total scores of the two forms (A and B) constitutes the individual's score of intelligence.

Description of Children's Embedded Figures Test

Children's Embedded Figure Test (CEFT) developed by Stephen A Karp and Norma Konstadt and published by Consulting Psychologists Press is a performance test for measuring cognitive style of children in the 5 to 12 year age range.

The CEFT is a perceptual test. The subject's task on each trial is to locate a previously seen simple figure within a larger complex figure which has been so organized as to obscure or embed the sought-after simple figure. Performance on the CEFT reflects the extent of competence at perceptual disembedding.

Responses against test series are scored 1 or 0. A score 1 is given only when the first choice is correct. If an incorrect choice is spontaneously corrected before the child sees the cut-out model, full credit is given. Correct choices made after the model is seen are scored as failures. The total score equals the number of items passed, 25 being the maximum score.

Collection of Data

The measurement of Academic Achievement followed by the measurement of creativity, Intelligence and cognitive style were done in succession in each of the schools under consideration.

The test responses were scored according to the principles and directions given in the respective manuals.

3

Data: Its Analysis

Organization of Scores

The raw scores were recorded separately for all variables against individual sample. Instead of using composite (global) scores of creativity, the raw scores of the constituent measures of creativity were recorded separately as figural fluency (FIG FLU), figural flexibility (FIG FLEX), figural originality (FIG ORI), figural elaboration (FIG ELA), verbal fluency (VER FLU), verbal flexibility (VER FLEX) and verbal originality (VER ORI) to study the issues under investigation at depth. The raw scores of intelligence (INT) were computed by taking the average of the total scores obtained by individual sample on two parallel forms of intelligence tests. The raw scores of cognitive style (COGS), academic achievement in Mathematics (MATH) and Bengali (BENG) were also recorded.

Thus, the raw scores recorded against individual sample were eleven in number such as FIG FLU, FIG FLEX, FIG ORI,FIG ELA, VER FLU, VER FLEX, VER ORI, INT, COGS, MATH and BENG.

Means and Standard Deviations of Criterion and Predictor Variables

The raw scores on different variables (both criterions and predictors) obtained by the sample (N=505) were arranged in frequency distributions. The mean and standard deviations on these variables were computed. The statistics have been shown in Table 10.

Table 10. Mean and S.D. of Criterion and Predictor Variables

Sl. No.	*Variables*	*Mean*	*S.D*
1	FIG FLU	15.39	6.16
2	FIG FLEX	12.27	4.37
3	FIG ORI	13.46	7.45
4	FIG ELA	19.18	12.38
5	VER FLU	19.38	8.85
6	VER FLEX	11.97	4.59
7	VER ORI	1.38	2.04
8	INT	16.41	5.34
9	COGS	9.44	4.59
10	MATH	16.38	9.59
11	BENG	31.24	12.84

Table 10 showed that the means and standard deviations of scores obtained by the sample (N = 505) on different variables under consideration were almost in conformity with the values stated in the manuals of respective tests.

Determination of Gender Differences in Mean Scores on all Variables

The analysis and interpretation by means of inferential statistics (t-test) have been presented here by taking into account the scores on all variables obtained by the boys and girls under consideration.

Table 11. Mean Differences between Boys and Girls on All Variables

Variables	*BOYS (N=308)*		*GIRLS (N=197)*		*t*
	Mean	*SD*	*Mean*	*SD*	*(df = 503)*
FIG FLU	16.78	5.77	13.22	6.15	6.52*
FIG FLEX	13.34	4.07	10.59	4.31	7.19*
FIG ORI	14.40	7.04	12.00	7.85	3.50*
FIG ELA	23.71	12.91	12.11	7.11	13.00*
VER FLU	21.57	9. 78	15.96	5.70	8.17*
VER FLEX	13.21	4.96	10.04	3.10	8.90*
VER ORI	1.90	2.40	0.60	0.86	8.76*
INT	17.26	5.64	15.10	4.62	4.78*
COGS	10.40	4.94	7.95	3.53	6.50*
MATH	18.24	11.05	13.50	5.60	6.42*
BENG	33.52	14.04	27.70	9.70	5.56*

* $P < .01$.

The results shown in the table 11 reveals that boys differed significantly from girls on each of the variables under consideration. An examination to the mean scores presented in Table 11 shows that mean scores of boys are higher than that of the girls on all variables. It indicates that the boys performed better than girls on all variables.

Graphical Representation of the Distributions of Scores

The mean scores obtained by the boys and girls on each variable have been presented graphically for visual comparison with the help of sets of paired columns drawn on the same axes.

Determination of Relationships between Criterion and Predictor Variables:

To study the relationship between academic achievement and other variables under consideration correlation techniques were followed in this study. The researcher computed Product Moment Correlation Coefficients separately for boys and girls between

(i) the academic achievement scores in Mathematics and the scores on each measure of creativity, intelligence and cognitive style

(ii) the academic achievement scores in Bengali and the scores on each measure of creativity, intelligence and cognitive style.

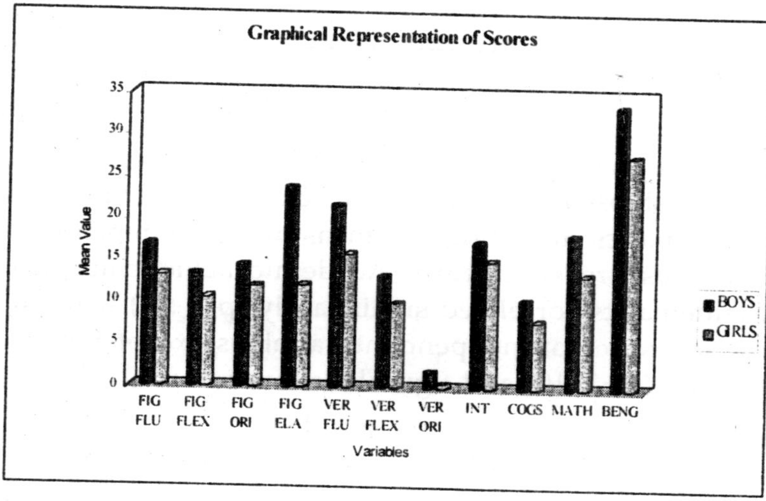

Determination of Relationship between the Scores of the Boys on Academic Achievement in Mathematics and Different Measures of Independent Variables

The coefficients of correlation between the scores of the boys on academic achievement in Mathematics and their scores on each measure of creativity, intelligence and cognitive style were computed and the said coefficients of correlations have been shown in Table 12.

Table 12. Relationship between the Scores of the Boys on Academic Achievement in Mathematics and Measures of Independent Variables

Sl. No.	*Measures of Creativity*	*Coefficient of Correlation (r)*
1.	FIG FLU	.10
2.	FIG FLEX	.18*
3.	FIG ORI	.22*
4.	FIG ELA	.08
5.	VER FLU	.47*
6.	VER FLEX	.39*
7.	VER ORI	.20*
8.	INT	.54*
9.	COGS	.38*

*P < .01 for df = 306

It is evident from Table 12 that most of the relationships between academic achievement of boys in mathematics and different measures of independent variables are significant. Academic achievement in Mathematics correlated significantly ($p < .01$) with all the measures of independent variables except figural fluency ($r = 0.10$) and figural elaboration ($r=0.08$).

Moreover, from the magnitude of the relationships as shown in Table 12 it is found that verbal measures of creative ability of the boys have much more influence on their academic achievement in Mathematics in comparison to the figural measures of creativity. Similarly intelligence has high positive co5rrelation with achievement in Mathematics. So, it can be inferred that the verbal fluency and intelligence of the boys seem to be the strongest cognitive components that help in their academic achievement in Mathematics.

Determination of Relationship between the Scores of the Boys on Academic Achievement in Bengali and Different Measures of Independent Variables:

The coefficients of correlation between the scores of the boys on academic achievement in Bengali and their scores on each measure of creativity, intelligence and cognitive style were computed and the said coefficients of correlations have been shown in Table 13.

Table 13. Relationship between the Scores of the Boys an Academic Achievement in Bengali and Different Measures of Independent Variables

Sl. No.	*Measures of Creativity*	*Coefficient of Correlation (r)*
1.	FIG FLU	.05
2.	FIG FLEX	.15*
3.	FIG ORI	.17*
4.	FIG ELA	.05
5.	VER FLU	.45*
6.	VER FLEX	.40*
7.	VER ORI	.15*
8.	INT	.59*
9.	COGS	.36*

*P < .01 for df = 306.

From Table 13 it is found that most of the relationships between academic achievement of the boys in Bengali and different measures independent variables are significant. Academic achievement in Bengali correlated significantly ($p < .01$) with all the measures of independent variables except figural fluency ($r = 0.05$) and figural elaboration ($r = 0.5$).

Again from the magnitude of relationships as shown in Table 13 it is found that of all the measures of creativity only verbal fluency showed the better relationship ($r = 0.45$) with academic achievement in Bengali. Similarly intelligence has high positive correlation with achievement in Bengali. So, it can be concluded that verbal fluency and intelligence of the boys seem to be the strongest components that help in their academic achievement in Bengali.

Determination of Relationship between the Scores of the Girls on Academic Achievement in Mathematics and Different Measures of Independent Variables

The product moment coefficients of correlation between the scores of the girls on academic achievement in Mathematics and their scores on each measure of independent variables were computed. The coefficients of correlation have been summarised in Table 14.

Table 14. Relationship between the Scores of the Girls on Academic Achievement in Mathematics and Different Measures of Independent Variables

Sl. No.	*Measures of Creativity*	*Coefficient of Correlation (r)*
1.	FIG FLU	.36*
2.	FIG FLEX	.38*
3.	FIG ORI	.35*
4.	FIG ELA	.26*
5.	VER FLU	.41*
6.	VER FLEX	.32*
7.	VER ORI	.20*
8.	INT	.33*
9.	COGS	.25*

*P < .01 for df = 195

From Table 14 it is found that most of the relationships between academic achievement of the girls in Mathematics and different measures of independent variables are significant (p < .01). It is obvious that the creative abilities, intelligence and cognitive style of the girls act positively to favour their academic achievement in Mathematics.

Again the magnitude of relationships shown in Table 14 indicates that of the measures of creativity only verbal fluency showed better relationship (r = 0.41) with academic achievement in Mathematics. Verbal fluency of the girls seems to be the most influential component of creativity that helps in their academic achievement in Mathematics.

Determination of Relationship between the Scores of the Girls on Academic Achievement in Bengali and Different Measures of Independent Variables

The product moment coefficients of correlation between the scores of the girls on academic achievement in Bengali and their scores on each measure of creativity were computed. The coefficients of correlation have been summarised in Table 15.

Table 15. Relationship between the Scores of the Girls on Academic Achievement in Bengali and Different Measures of Independent Variables

Sl. No.	*Measures of Creativity*	*Coefficient of Correlation (r)*
1.	FIG FLU	.36*
2.	FIG FLEX	.36*
3.	FIG ORI	.35*
4.	FIG ELA	.36*
5.	VER FLU	.40*
6.	VER FLEX	.27*
7.	VER ORI	.18**
8.	INT	.28*
9.	COGS	.19*

**p < .05, *P < .01 for df = 195

From Table 15 it is found that the relationships between academic achievement of the girls in Bengali and different measures of independent variables are significant. (P < .05 & p < .01). Since all the measures of creativity, intelligence and cognitive style correlated positively and significantly with academic achievement in Bengali, it is clear that they play positive role in their academic achievement girls in Bengali.

Again the magnitude of relationships shown in Table 15 it is found that the measures of creativity only verbal fluency showed better relationship (r = .40) with academic achievement in Bengali. Verbal fluency of the girls seems to be the strongest component of creativity that helps in their academic achievement in Bengali.

Summary of Inter correlations among Predictor Variables and Criterion Variables

The summary of the inter correlations obtained among the predictor variables (creativity, intelligence and cognitive style) and the criterion variables (academic achievement in Mathematics and Bengali) has been presented separately for the boys and girls in the form of a inter correlation matrix (11 x 11) in Tables 16 and 17.

Multiple Regression and Multiple Correlation

The most useful approach o the prediction of a given variable is multiple regression, in which the estimate of the criterion measure is based on the linear combination of the several independent variables. For example, the academic achievement (Y), the criterion, may be predicted from a linear combination of such variables (predictors) as figural fluency (X_1), figural flexibility (X_2), figural originality (X_3), figural elaboration (X_4), verbal fluency (X_5), verbal flexibility (X_6), verbal originality (X_7), intelligence (X_8) and cognitive style(X_9) through an equation of the form

$$Y = ß_1X_1 + ß_2X_2 + ß_3X_3 + ß_4X_4 + ß_5X_5 + ß_6X_6 + ß_7X_7 + ß_8X_8 + ß_9X_9 + k \quad \ldots \quad (1)$$

Table 16. Intercorrelation among the Predictor Variables for the Boys

Sl. No.	*Variables*	*(1)*	*(2)*	*(3)*	*(4)*	*(5)*	*(6)*	*(7)*	*(8)*	*(9)*	*(10)*	*(11)*
(1)	FIG FLU	1.00	.83**	.61**	.50**	.19**	.16**	.13**	.16**	18**	10	.05
(2)	FIG FLEX		1.00	.69**	.50**	.24**	.24**	.14**	.22**	.20**	.18**	.15**
(3)	FIG ORI			1.00	.57**	.23**	.25**	.16**	.24**	.22**	.22**	.17**
(4)	FIG ELA				1.00	.21**	.23**	.26**	.21**	.25**	.08	.05
(5)	VER FLU					1.00	.87**	.57**	.51**	.54**	.47**	.45**
(6)	VER FLEX						1.00	.55**	.45**	.49**	.39**	.40**
(7)	VER ORI							1.00	.30**	.43**	.20**	.15**
(8)	INT								1.00	.56*	.54**	.59**
(9)	COGS									1.00	.38**	.36**
(10)	MATH										1.00	.69**
(11)	BENG											1.00

* P<.05, ** P <.01 for df = 306

Table 17. Intercorrelation among the Predictor Variables for the Girls

Sl. No.	*Variables*	*(1)*	*(2)*	*(3)*	*(4)*	*(5)*	*(6)*	*(7)*	*(8)*	*(9)*	*(10)*	*(11)*
(1)	FIG FLU	1.00	.91**	.75**	.48**	.51**	.39**	.19**	.38**	.41**	.36**	.36**
(2)	FIG FLEX		1.00	.79**	.49**	.44**	.35**	.21**	.36**	35**	.38**	.36**
(3)	FIG ORI			1.00	.50**	.35**	.22**	.15**	.28**	35**	.35**	.35**
(4)	FIG ELA				1.00	.31**	.33**	.16**	.31**	.30**	.26**	.36**
(5)	VER FLU					1.00	.79**	.46**	.33**	.41**	.41**	.40**
(6)	VER FLEX						1.00	.50**	.35**	.26**	.32**	.27**
(7)	VER ORI							1.00	.12	.12	.20**	.18**
(8)	INT								1.00	53*	.33**	.28**
(9)	COGS									1.00	.25**	.19**
(10)	MATH										1.00	.36**
(11)	BENG											1.00

* P<.05 ** P <.01 for df = 195

Where, the beta multipliers of the independent variables known as regression coefficients are to be computed to maximize the prediction of the dependent variables and k is known as constant or intercept which makes appropriate adjustments for differences between the means of criterion and predictor variables.

The regression coefficients B_1, B_2 etc. give the weights to be attached to the scores in each of the independent variable (X_1, X_2 .... etc.), when the dependent variable (Y) is to be estimated from all of these combinations. Moreover, these regression coefficients give the weights which each variable exerts in determining Y when the influence of the other variable is excluded.

Now the accuracy of the multiple regression equation as a predicting instrument is given by the coefficient of multiple correlation. It indicates the correlation between a set of obtained scores and the same scores predicted from the multiple regression equation. In other words, multiple correlation gives the correlation between a criterion and a team of predictors. It is designated by the letter R and readily computed from the beta coefficients by way of equation.

$$R^2_{1(23456789)} = \beta_{12.3456789} r_{12} + \beta_{13.2456789} r_{13} + \beta_{14.2356789} r_{14} + \beta_{15.2346789} r_{15} + \beta_{16.2345789} r_{16} + \beta_{17.2345689} r_{17} + \beta_{18.2345679} r_{18} + \beta_{19.2345678} r_{19}$$

where, $\beta_{12.3456789}$, $\beta_{13.2456789}$ ... etc, are the regression coefficients and r_{12}, r_{13} ... etc are the product moment coefficients of correlation between the scores on criterion and predictor variables.

Thus the researcher applied multiple regression procedures simultaneously with all nine predictor variables (FIG FLU, FIG FLEX, FIG ORI, FIG ELA, VER FLU, VER FLEX, VER ORI, INT and COGS) to predict

(i) academic achievement of the boys in Mathematics,
(ii) academic achievement of the boys in Bengali,
(iii) academic achievement of the girls in Mathematics and
(iv) academic achievement of the girls in Bengali.

The multiple correlation (R) was also computed in each case.

Prediction of Academic Achievement of the Boys in Mathematics

The result of the multiple regression of academic achievement of the boys in Mathematics simultaneously with all nine predictor variables has been shown in Table 18.

Table 18. Multiple Regression of Academic Achievement in Mathematics Simultaneously with all the Predictor Variables for the Boys (N = 308)

Predictor Variable	*beta (ß)*	*t*	*p*
FIG FLU	-0.11	-1.26	< .21
FIG FLEX	0.07	0.77	< .44
FIG ORI	0.14	2.00	< .04
FIG ELA	-0.10	-1.73	< .08
VER FLU	0.40	3.97	<.00
VER FLEX	-0.11	- 1.19	<.23

VER ORI	-0.09	-1.61	< .11
INT	0.38	6.45	< .00
COGS	0.05	0.85	< .39

Multiple R^2 = 0.37, F (9,298) = 19.83, p < .00
Multiple R = 0.61, p < .01
Intercept = - 1.55

Now substituting the different ß values from Table 18 in equation (1) the regression equation for prediction of academic achievement in Mathematics (Y) of the boys from the combination of all the predictor variables takes the form as given below:

$$Y = -0.11X_1 + 0.07X_2 + 0.14X_3 - 0.10X_4 + 0.40X_5 - 0.11X_6 - 0.09X_7 + 0.38X_8 + 0.05X_9 - 1.55$$

From Table 18 it is clear that the repression procedure resulted in a R^2 of 0.37, F (9,298) = 19.83, p < .00. It indicates that about 37% of variance of academic achievement in Mathematics was explained jointly by different measures of creativity, intelligence and cognitive style of the boys under consideration. Moreover, the multiple correlation (R) between academic achievement in Mathematics and figural fluency, figural flexibility, figural originality, figural elaboration, verbal fluency, verbal flexibility, verbal originality, intelligence cognitive style of the boys was found to be 0.61 which was significant at .01 level. So the measure of creativity, intelligence and cognitive style of the boys combined together is a good predictor of their academic achievement in Mathematics.

The researcher decided to apply stepwise multiple regression procedure to determine which variables were important predictors of academic achievement of the boys in Mathematics across the nine predictor variables. The variable selection method first determined the best one-variable model (i.e., the single variable that best correlated with academic achievement in Mathematics). Then the best two-variable model was selected on the basis of maximum R^2 improvement. This process continued by determining the best three variable model yielding the largest R^2 improvement, and so forth, until a model containing all the variables as predictors of academic achievement of the boys in Mathematics was generated. To determine the size of the best model to select, it was decided to choose the last one in which the increment in R^2 was significant. The result of the stepwise regression has been summarized in Table 19.

Table 19. Stepwise Multiple Regression of Academic Achievement in Mathematics with the Predictor Variables for the Boys (N=308)

Step No.	*Variable entered*	*R^2*	*Change in R^2*	*F*
1.	INT	.291	.291	125.78**
2.	+ VER FLU	.346	.055	25.54**
3.	+ VER ORI	.354	.008	4.14*
4.	+ FIG ORI	.359	.005	2.03
5.	+ FIG ELA	.367	.008	3.79
6.	+ VER FLEX	.369	.002	1.14
7.	+ FIG FLU	.371	.002	0.98
8.	+ COGS	.373	.002	0.69
9.	+ FIG FLEX	.374	.001	0.59

*P < .05 ** P < .01

From Table 19 it is clear that the stepwise regression procedure applied to the boys (N=308) yielded step 3, the three variable solution, in which the increment in R^2 is significant at .05 level. The three variable solution for the boys has been presented in Table 20.

Table 20. Model of Best Prediction of Academic Achievement in Mathematics for the Boys (N = 308)

Predictor Variable	*beta (ß)*	*F*	*P*
INT	.40	57.04	< .00
VER FLU	.33	29.23	< .00
VER ORI	-.11	4.14	< .05

Multiple R = 0.35, F (3,304) = 55.74, p < .00

Intercept = - 2.60

The findings showed that three variables were best predictors and that all contributed statistically to the variance of the academic achievement of the boys in Mathematics. Two of the variables, intelligence and verbal fluency, had positive parameter estimates. The third variable verbal originality had a negative parameter estimate.

It is also found that the three variables solution resulted in a R^2 of 0.35, F (3,304) = 55.74, p < .00 which was not substantially lower than the R^2 of 0.37 (Table 18) for the multiple regression procedure applied simultaneously with all nine predictor variables.

Since the various weightings of variables contributing to the prediction of academic achievement of the boys in Mathematics were of interest, it was found that intelligence of the boys made the largest contribution to the prediction of the variance of their academic achievement in Mathematics in presence of the remaining two variables in the model, with a beta of 0.40. The verbal fluency measure of the boys contributed less than the intelligence measure to the prediction of the variance of their achievement in Mathematics in the presence of the remaining two variables in the model, with a beta of 0.33. But it contributed more than the verbal originality measure which had a negative beta value of – 0.11. An explanation to account for the presence of the verbal originality measure in the best prediction model and its negative parameter estimate is that this variable may serve as a moderator variable. Zedeck (1971) suggests that a moderator variable effects the nature or degree of association between a criterion variable and a given correlate or set of correlates. Thus, verbal originality may serve as a variable that interacts with the other two variables in the model to enhance the predictability of academic achievement in Mathematics.

The obvious and simplest interpretation of the best prediction model is that the intelligence and virtually the verbal measures (fluency and originality) of creative thinking ability serve as the foundation for academic achievement of the boys in Mathematics.

Prediction of Academic Achievement of the Boys in Bengali

The result of the multiple regression of academic achievement of the boys in Bengali simultaneously with all nine predictor variables has been shown in Table 21.

Table 21. Multiple Regression of Academic Achievement in Bengali Simultaneously with all the Predictor Variables for the Boys (N = 308)

Predictor Variable	*beta (ß)*	*t*	*p*
FIG FLU	-0.17	- 2.16	<.03
FIG FLEX	0.14	1.54	<.12
FIG ORI	0.08	1.20	<.23
FIG ELA	- 0.11	-1.87	<.06
VER FLU	0.21	2.20	<.03
VER FLEX	- 0.08	- 0.85	<.40
VER ORI	- 0.15	- 2.64	<.01
INT	0.48	8.61	<.00
COGS	0.01	0.17	<.86

Multiple R^2 = 0.41, F (9,298) = 23.50, $p < .00$
Multiple R = 0.64, $p < .01$
Intercept = - 5.81

Now substituting the different ß values from Table 21 in equation (1) the regression equation for prediction of academic achievement in Bengali (Y) of the boys from the combination of all the predictor variables takes the form as given below:

$$Y = -0.17X_1 + 0.14X_2 + 0.08X_3 - 0.11X_4 + 0.21X_5 - 0.08X_6 - 0.15X_7 + 0.48X_8 + 0.01X_9 - 5.81$$

The result showed that the regression procedure yielded R^2 of 0.41, F (9,298) = 23.50, $p < .00$. It means that about 41% of variance of academic achievement in Bengali was explained jointly by different measures of creativity, intelligence and cognitive style of the boys under consideration. Moreover the multiple correlation (R) between academic achievement in Bengali and figural fluency, figural flexibility, figural originality, figural elaboration, verbal fluency, verbal flexibility, verbal originality, intelligence and cognitive style of the boys was found to be 0.64 which was significant at .01 level. So, the measure of creativity, intelligence and cognitive style of the boys combined together is a good predictor of their academic achievement in Bengali.

The researcher decided to apply stepwise multiple regression procedure to determine which variables were important predictors of academic achievement of the boys in Bengali across the nine predictor variables. The variable selection method was the same as adopted earlier. The result of the stepwise regression has been summarized in Table 22.

Table 22. Stepwise Multiple Regression of Academic Achievement in Bengali with the Predictor Variables for the Boys (N=308)

Step No.	*Variable entered*	*R^2*	*Change in R^2*	*F*
1.	INT	.346	.346	161.93**
2.	+ VER FLU	.375	.029	14.42**
3.	+ VER ORI	.394	.019	9.32**
4.	+ FIG ORI	.399	.005	2.91
5.	+ FIG ELA	.403	.004	1.95
6.	+ VER FLEX	.408	.005	2.51
7.	+ FIG FLU	.413	.005	2.54
8.	+ COGS	.415	.002	0.73
9.	+ FIG FLEX	.415	.000	0.00

** $P < .01$

From Table 22 it is clear that the stepwise regression procedure applied to the boys (N-308) yielded step 3, the three variable solution, in which the increment in R^2 is significant at .01 level. The three variable solution for the boys has been presented in Table 23.

Table 23. Model of Best Prediction of Academic Achievement in Bengali for the Boys (N = 308)

Predictor Variable	*beta (ß)*	*F*	*P*
INT	.49	89.26	< .00
VER FLU	.29	23.70	< .00
VER ORI	-.16	9.32	< .01

Multiple $R^2 = 0.39$, $F(3,304) = 65.93$, $p < .00$

Intercept = - 5.25

The findings showed that three variables were best predictors and that all contributed statistically to the variance of the academic achievement of the boys in Bengali. Two of the variables, intelligence and verbal fluency, had positive parameter estimates. The third variable verbal originality had a negative parameter estimate.

The findings also suggested that the three variables solution resulted in a R^2 of 0.39, $F(3,304) = 65.93$, $p < .00$ which was not substantially lower than the R^2 of 0.41 (Table 21) for the multiple regression procedure applied simultaneously with all nine predictor variables.

The best prediction model showed that intelligence of the boys made the largest contribution to the prediction of the variance of their academic achievement in Bengali in presence of the remaining two variables, with a beta of 0.49. The verbal fluency measure of the boys contributed less than the intelligence measure to the prediction of the variance of their academic achievement in Bengali in the presence of the remaining two variables in the model, with a beta of 0.29. But it contributed more than the verbal originality measure which had a negative beta of – 0.16. Verbal originality may serve as a moderator variable (Zedeck, 1971) that interacts with the other two variables in the model to enhance the predictability of academic achievement in Bengali.

Thus it can be interpreted that intelligence and two verbal measures (fluency and originality) of creative thinking ability serve as the foundation for academic achievement of the boys in Bengali. The similar interpretation was drawn in case of their academic achievement in Mathematics also.

Prediction of Academic Achievement of the Girls in Mathematics

The result of the multiple regression of academic achievement of the girls in Mathematics simultaneously with all nine predictor variables has been shown in Table 24.

Table 24. Multiple Regression of Academic Achievement in Mathematics Simultaneously with all the Predictor Variables for the Girls (N = 197)

Predictor Variable	*beta (ß)*	*t*	*p*
FIG FLU	-0.14	- 0.87	< .38
FIG FLEX	0. 21	1.25	< .21
FIG ORI	0.13	1.16	< .25

FIG ELA	-0.03	- 0.41	< .68
VER FLU	0.34	2.97	<. 00
VER FLEX	-0.08	- 0.71	<. 48
VER ORI	-0.02	- 0.31	< .76
INT	0.20	2.56	< .01
COGS	0.05	0.57	< .57

Multiple $R^2 = 0.26$, $F(9,298) = 7.20$, $p < .00$

Multiple R = 0.51, $p < .01$

Intercept = - 3.75

Now substituting the different ß values from Table 24 in equation (1) the regression equation for prediction of academic achievement in Mathematics (Y) of the girls from the combination of all the predictor variables takes the form as given below:

$$Y = -0.14X_1 + 0.21X_2 + 0.13X_3 - 0.03X_4 + 0.34X_5 - 0.08X_6 - 0.02X_7 + 0.20X_8 + 0.05X_9 - 3.75$$

From Table 24 it is clear that he regression procedure resulted in a R^2 of 0.26, $F(9,187) = 7.20$, $p < .00$. It indicates that about 26% of variance of academic achievement in Mathematics was explained jointly by different measures of creativity, intelligence and cognitive style of the girls under consideration. Moreover the multiple correlation (R) between academic achievement in Mathematics and figural fluency, figural flexibility, figural originality, figural elaboration, verbal fluency, verbal flexibility, verbal originality, intelligence, cognitive style of the girls was found to be 0.51 which was significant at .01 level. So the measure of creativity, intelligence and cognitive style of the girls combined together is a good predictor of their academic achievement in Mathematics.

The researcher decided to apply stepwise multiple regression procedure to determine which variables were important predictors of academic achievement of the girls in Mathematics across the nine predictor variables. The variable selection method was the same as adopted in earlier cases. The result of the stepwise regression has been summarized in Table 25.

Table 25. Stepwise Multiple Regression of Academic Achievement in Mathematics with the Predictor Variables for the Girls (N=197)

Step No.	*Variable entered*	*R^2*	*Change in R^2*	*F*
1.	INT	.171	.171	40.36**
2.	+ VER FLU	.220	.051	12.09**
3.	+ VER ORI	.244	.024	6.28**
4.	+ FIG ORI	.250	.006	1.48
5.	+ FIG ELA	.254	.004	0.96
6.	+ VER FLEX	.255	.001	0.25
7.	+ FIG FLU	.256	.001	0.30
8.	+ COGS	.257	.001	0.17
9.	+ FIG FLEX	.257	.000	0.09

*p < .05 ** P < .01

From Table 25 it is found that the stepwise regression procedure applied to the girls (N = 197) yielded step 3, the three variable solution, in which the increment in R^2 is significant at .05 level. The three variable solution for the girls has been presented in Table 26.

Table 26. Model of Best Prediction of Academic Achievement in Mathematics for the Girls (N = 197)

Predictor Variable	*beta (ß)*	*F*	*P*
VER FLU	.27	14.22	< .00
FIG FLEX	.19	7.65	< .01
INT	.17	6.28	< .05

Multiple R^2 = 0.24, F (3,193) = 20.84, p < .00

Intercept = - 3.33

The findings showed that the three variables were best predictors and that all contributed statistically to the variance of academic achievement of the girls in Mathematics. The three variable solution resulted in a R^2 of 0.24, F (3.193) = 20.84, p < .00 which was not substantially lower than the R^2 of 0.26 (Table 24) for the multiple regression procedure applied simultaneously with all the nine predictor variables. The best prediction model showed that verbal fluency of the girls made the largest contribution to the prediction of the variance of their academic achievement in Mathematics in presence of the remaining two variables, with a beta of 0.27. The figural flexibility measure of the girls contributed less than verbal fluency measure in presence of the remaining two variables (VER FLU and INT) in the model, with a beta of 0.19. The smallest contribution made by the intelligence measure of the girls to the prediction of the variance of their academic achievement in Mathematics in presence of the remaining two variables (VER FLU and FIG FLEX) in the model, with a beta of 0.17.

Thus, the simplest interpretation is that verbal fluency and figural flexibility measures of creative thinking ability and intelligence serve as the foundation for academic achievement of the girls in Mathematics.

Prediction of Academic Achievement of the Girls in Bengali

The result of the multiple regression of academic achievement of the girls in Bengali simultaneously with all nine predictor variables has been shown in Table 27.

Table 27. Multiple Regression of Academic Achievement in Bengali Simultaneously with all the Predictor Variables for the Girls (N = 197)

Predictor Variable	*beta (ß)*	*t*	*p*
FIG FLU	-0.01	-0.06	< .95
FIG FLEX	0.01	0.07	< .94
FIG ORI	0.12	1.16	< .25
FIG ELA	-0.21	-2.76	< .01
VER FLU	0.43	3.70	<. 00
VER FLEX	-0.21	-1.86	<. 06
VER ORI	-0.03	-0.42	< .68
INT	0.17	2.18	< .03
COGS	0.14	-1.69	< .09

Multiple R^2 = 0.27, F (9,187) = 7.62, $p < .00$
Multiple R = 0.52, $p < .01$
Intercept = - 14.14

Now substituting the different ß values from Table 27 in equation (1) the regression equation for prediction of academic achievement in Bengali (Y) of the girls from the combination of all the predictor variables takes the form as given below :

$$Y = -0.01X_1 + 0.01X_2 + 0.12X_3 - 0.21X_4 + 0.43X_5 - 0.21X_6 - 0.03X_7 + 0.17X_8 + 0.14X_9 - 14.14$$

From the above table, it is clear that the regression procedure result in R^2 of 0.27, F (9,187) = 7.62, $p < .00$. It indicates that about 27% of variance of academic achievement in Bengali was explained jointly by different measures of creativity, intelligence and cognitive style of the girls under consideration. Moreover the multiple correlation (R) between academic achievement in Bengali and figural fluency, figural flexibility, figural originality, figural verbal fluency, verbal flexibility, verbal originality, intelligence and cognitive style of the girls was found to be 0.52 which was significant at .01 level. So the measure of creativity, intelligence and cognitive style of the girls combined together is a good predictor of their academic achievement in Bengal.

The researcher applied, stepwise multiple regression procedure to determine which variables were important predictors of academic achievement of the girls in Bengali across the nine predictor variables. The variable selection method was the same as adopted earlier. The result of the stepwise regression has been summarized in Table 28.

Table 28. Stepwise Multiple Regression of Academic Achievement in Bengali with the Predictor Variables for the Girls (N=197)

Step No.		*Variable entered*	R^2	*Change in* R^2	*F*
1.		INT	.157	.157	36.38**
2.	+	VER FLU	.221	.064	16.10**
3.	+	VER ORI	.239	.018	4.49**
4.	+	FIG ORI	.247	.008	2.00
5.	+	FIG ELA	.256	.009	2.25
6.	+	VER FLEX	.267	.011	2.98
7.	+	FIG FLU	.268	.001	0.18
8.	+	COGS	.268	.000	0.00
9.	+	FIG FLEX	.268	.000	0.00

*p < .05, ** P < .01

From Table 48 it is found that the stepwise regression procedure applied to the girls (N=197) yielded step 3, the three variable solution, in which the increment in R^2 is significant at .05 level. The three variable solution for the girls has been presented in Table 29.

Table 29. Model of Best Prediction of Academic Achievement in Bengali for the Girls (N = 197)

Predictor Variable	*beta (ß)*	*F*	*P*
VER FLU	.28	16.77	< .00
FIG FLEX	.19	7.35	< .01
INT	.15	4.49	< .05

Multiple R^2 = 0.24, F (3,193) = 20.26, p < .00

Intercept = - 14.42

The findings showed that the three variables were best predictors and that all contributed statistically to the variance of academic achievement of the girls in Bengali. The three variable solution resulted in a R^2 of 0.24, F (3.193) = 20.26, p < .00 which was not substantially lower than the R^2 of 0.27 (Table 27) for the multiple regression procedure applied simultaneously with all the nine predictor variables. The best prediction model showed that verbal fluency of the girls made the largest contribution to the prediction of the variance of their academic achievement in Bengali in presence of the remaining two variables, with a beta of 0.28. The figural elaboration measure of the girls contributed less than verbal fluency measure of the remaining two variables (VER FLU and FIG ORI) in the model, with a beta of 0.19. The smallest contribution made by figural originality measure of the girls to the prediction of the variance of their academic achievement in Bengali in presence of the remaining two variables (VER FLU and FIG ELA) in the model, with a beta of 0.15.

Thus, the simplest interpretation is that verbal fluency and figural flexibility measures of creative thinking ability and intelligence serve as the foundation for academic achievement of the girls in Bengali.

Summary of the Best Prediction Models

The summary of the results of different best prediction models obtained has been presented in Table 30.

Table 30. Summary of the Best Prediction Models

Groups	*Boys (N=308)*			*Girls (N=197)*		
Criterion	*Best predictors*	*beta (β)*	R^2	*Best predictors*	*beta (β)*	R^2
1. Academic	INT	.40*		VER FLU	.27*	
Achievement in	VER FLU	.33*	.35*	FIG FLEX	.19*	.24*
Mathematics	VER ORI	-.11**		INT	.17**	
2. Academic	INT	.49*		VER FLU	.28*	
Achievement in	VER FLU	.29*	.39*	FIG FLEX	.19*	.24*
Bengali	VER ORI	-.16**		INT	.15**	

*$p < .01$, **$p < .05$.

4

Discussion

Discussion of the Results

In this study the researcher intended to study the relationship of academic achievement (criterion) with creativity, intelligence and cognitive style (predictors) of primary school children. In doing so, the scores obtained by the subjects on these variables were organized into frequency distributions. The data were analyzed by employing t-test, correlation techniques and multiple regression for testing the hypotheses framed.

On the basis of the analysis and interpretation of data made in the previous chapter, the researcher attempts to discuss here the findings of the study to ascertain the extent to which these results are useful in throwing light on the research problem raised in the first chapter and also to link them with the empirical findings in the specific areas with which this investigation was concerned.

1. The present study aimed at determining if there was any significant difference between the boys and girls of Class IV with regard to creativity, intelligence, cognitive style, and academic achievement in Mathematics and Bengali.

(a) With regard to creativity, it has been found in Table 11 that the boys have differed significantly ($p < .01$) from the girls on all measures of creative thinking ability. The mean scores of the boys on all measures (FIG FLU, FIG FLEX, FIG ORI, FIG ELA, VER FLU, VER FLEX, VER ORI) are found higher than that of the girls. It may, therefore, be said that boys in general are having creative thinking ability more than that of the girls. This finding of the present study is supported by the studies of Raina (1968, 1969), Prakash (1966), Ganeja (1972) and Tara (1981) with Indian students, Kelly (1965) found that fourth grade girls scored significantly lower than did fourth grade boys on the non-verbal creativity measures. Strans and Strans (1968) reported that girls' scores were lower than those of boys in both Indian and American societies while sex differences in creativity were greatest in India.

Contrary to the present finding several investigators reported superiority of females over males in creative thinking. Ogletree (1971) reported that girls excelled boys significantly on all creativity measures, both verbal and figural. Passi (1972) obtained superiority of girls to boys on non-verbal creativity. Kim at el (1965) found that Korean high school females exhibited higher average levels of performance on creativity tests than their male counterparts. The present findings showing significant gender differences in favour of the boys on all measures of creative thinking ability may be explained in the following way.

The direction in which the intellectual potentialities of children, whatever be their levels of potentiality, are developed (towards convergence or divergence), is at least partly, guided by the kinds of interactions the children have with their parents. The parents' thinking about how children should be treated is, in turn, related to the way in which they themselves were reared and, in fact, to the prevailing cultural notions about what is right and what wrong behaviour in children. If a culture imposes severe negative sanctions against certain behaviours, most parents will try to suppress them in their children, while they will foster those behaviours which the culture approves.

The behavioural traits like adventurous, unorthodox, unwilling to accept authority, likely to ask awkward questions, humorous and the like may sometimes be valued in boys and, in fact, are usually highly admired out of the classroom but they are seldom valued in girls. On the contrary, even in these days of emancipation, sex equality and the like, the values accepted as characterizing females, and most desirable in females, tend to be more concerned with meekness being a lady (i.e., conforming), being well-behaved (with respect to the social code) and so on. Unorthodox is, even today in India, far more reprehensible in females than males, and the accepted behavioural norms for girls are considerably less favourable to divergent thinking than are those for boys. So conformity is taught from birth to the girls of major portion of Indian Territory. Our over emphasis or misplaced emphasis on sex roles and efforts to establish sex norms during early childhood and throughout the educational ladder makes many problems for highly creative children. Torrance (1962) observed that concerns about sex appropriateness and emphasis on sex differences become tremendously inhibiting at about age five and continue into the beginning of the first grade. Hence if those qualities which are usually associated with the disposition towards creativity are almost universally frowned on in girls, it is scarcely surprising that few of them manage to develop in to divergent thinkers. Thus it may be conceived that sex differences in creative behaviour are more likely to result from the different cultural values applied to boys' and girls' behaviour than from innate female inferiority.

(b) With regard to intelligence, it has been found in Table 11 that the boys have differed significantly ($p < .01$) from the girls on the measure of intelligence. The mean score of the boys on the measure of intelligence is found to be higher than that of the girls. It indicates that the boys are more intelligent than the girls. This finding is in agreement with the finding obtained by Dixit (1985). In Dixit's study intelligence test scores of adolescent boys were significantly higher than those of adolescent girls. Contrary to the present finding Roach (1985) found that females demonstrated higher intelligence than the males. Besides these, many studies reported no difference between boys and girls on the measure of intelligence. Acharyulu (1978) found no significant sex difference in intelligence and Rastogi (1987) also reported no difference between boys and girls on intelligence score. The superiority of the boys as is found in the present study, over the girls on intelligence may be explained in the following way.

In the male dominated Indian society, boys are encouraged to become independent and self-supportive in all walks of life in comparison to their counterparts. They are usually rained to work independently, share experiences with others, and take part in free discussions and arguments and the like. In fact, the boys enjoy autonomy, self direction, spontaneity which, in turn, help them to expand the horizon of free and logical thinking. But girls of our society, on the other hand, do not usually get opportunity to have such type of experiences. Their life styles, even their expressions are controlled mostly by their counterparts. In this sense the girls of Indian society are culturally disadvantaged group. Because of being disadvantaged, typical intellectual characteristics, as observed by frost and Hawkes (1966), may develop within the girls—the important of which are anti intellectual attitude, fear of being ridiculed, feeling of alienation and inadequacy, inability to abstract, classify and conceptualize data, low ability to see cause and effect, negative self image as problem solver, quick and premature closer, preference for familiar, little or no experience in setting and proceeding to goals, poor performance on speeded or timed tests etc.

All these characteristics may consequently decelerate development of intelligence of the girls as compared to that of the boys in Indian society.

(c) With regard to cognitive style, it has been found in Table 11 that the boys have differed significantly ($p < .01$) from the girls on the measure of cognitive style. The mean score of the boys on the measure of cognitive style is found to be higher than that of the girls. It means that the boys have more ability than the girls in perceiving an embedded figure in a complex context. This finding finds support from the previous studies made by Bennett (1956), Witt (1955), Kato (1965), Dawson (1967), Okonji (1969).Consistent sex differences have repeatedly been found in all these studies where boys and men tend to be more field independent than girls and women. The present researcher (1997) also obtained the same finding in his earlier study.

Contrary to the present finding, Roach (1985) reported the superiority of the girls over the boys on the measure of cognitive style.

Explanation to the present finding may be made in the following way. One possible source of sex difference may be the early experiences of a child in a family. The proposition derived from cross cultural studies by Witkin (1978) and Berry (1991) suggested that children in group oriented cultures which socialize for dependence and conformity will have perceptual skills that are holistic and will view complex fields as integral wholes. Field independent children, in contrast tend to excel in perceptual disembedding tasks and their analytical cognitive style tends to reflect socialization for group independence. In India, girls are reared and socialized for dependence and conformity with a discouraging attitude towards autonomous functioning as compared to their counterparts. So, girls are expected to exhibit poor performance in perceptual disembedding tasks.

Besides this socialization experiences as origin of field dependence independence construct, differences in constitutional characteristics may come into play as suggested by different investigators. A large body of evidence relating differences in field dependence to differences in central nervous system and autonomic nervous system function has been reviewed by Witkin and Oltman (1967). Studies with infants suggest that some of the somatic differences found later in life may be present in the neonatal period and constitute precursors in the development of more differented or less differentiated functioning (Dyk, 1969). But definite conclusion regarding the underlying causes (genetic, social or psychological) that can explain a greater amount of variance in perceptual-disembedding skills of children, has not yet been drawn. Further researches in this direction need to continue.

(d) With regard to academic achievement in Mathematics, it has been found to Table 11 that the boys differed significantly ($p <.01$) from the girls. The superiority of the boys over the girls in academic achievement in mathematics indicates that the boys are more efficient in solving mathematical problems than the girls. The present finding is supported by the study of Marshall and Smith (1987). But Acharyulu (1978) found superiority of the girls over the boys on achievement in Mathematics. Mainks (1983) observed no sex difference in the acquisition of mathematical concepts.

However, the explanation to the present finding may be made in the following way.

Girls may be more likely than boys to have ability to automatize procedures of computation. Girls have the greater capacity in routinising well-defined procedural tasks, such as addition, subtraction etc. Such automaticity may occur without underlying conceptual development. So what happens when a word problem is encountered? As there is no explicit clue for operation one must evaluate the words in the problem to determine which operation/operations to carry out. This activation depends on the associations linking various bits of knowledge together, for example, decision about way to use an operation and what different steps in the operation mean, will lead to construction of a large network of knowledge. This net work is richer in conceptual understanding and contains a greater number of concepts and procedures. Consequently there are more paths leading to the correct procedures of computation.

As boys receive additional information from teachers, parents and societies (because of biological or social or cultural circumstances), they have greater scope to become informative and logical in approach in comparison to their counterparts. As such they do not apparently routinize procedures for carrying out arithmetic operations as the girls usually do. So the performance of the boys in arithmetic becomes better than that of the girls.

(e) With regard to academic achievement in Bengali, it has been found in Table 11 hat the boys have differed significantly ($p <.01$) from the girls. The mean score of the boys on academic achievement in Bengali is found to be higher than that of the girls. It indicates that the boys are more efficient in Bengali (Vernacular language) than the girls. The present finding is supported by the earlier study made by the present researcher (1997). Contrary to the present finding the study made by Mitra et al. (1995) showed a nonsignificant superiority of girls over boys in academic achievement in Bengali. The difference in findings of the present study from the findings of the above study may be attributed to the difference in the nature of the sample used. Research studies dealing with achievement in Bengali were too few to cite. However, the general trend, as observed by Dave (1988), indicates the poor performance of Indian primary school children (of grade IV) in language achievement.

The present finding may be explained in the following way.

Language occupies an important place in cognitive

development. The basic skills acquired through language learning facilitate learning of concepts in other areas. The basic language skills, namely, listening, speaking, reading, comprehension of ideas, language use, vocabulary control, functional grammar etc. get refined and modified through effective transactions in the day to day life situation. Boys of Indian society usually take part in communication at larger extent than their counter parts, with parents, teachers, peers and others at home, school and the society. Consequently they become more efficient in language and communication than the girls. On the other hand, the girls are usually trained to help the mother at home and to become efficient in house hold activities. Communication with the external world seems to be of secondary importance to them. Continuous dependency on the male members tends to refrain them from effective social transaction in all walks of life. This may make them gradually weaker in language competencies as compared to their counterparts.

(2) The present study attempted to investigate the relationship between academic achievement and creativity of primary school children of class IV. The researcher was confronted with the question- Are components of creative thinking ability of students related to their academic achievement?

In the present study it has been found that the academic achievement of both boys and girls in Mathematics and Bengali correlated significantly with different measures of their creative thinking ability (e.g. Figural fluency, flexibility, originality, elaboration and verbal fluency, flexibility, originally) (Tables 12, 13, 14 and 15). The figural fluency and figural elaboration measures of the boys failed to show significant relationships with academic achievement in both the subjects. This failure may be attributed to the nature of the sample. However, it can be interpreted in general hat the creative thinking ability of the students influenced their academic achievement.

The results of the present study are similar to those obtained by Torrance (1959), Cropley (1967) Sharma (1977), Singh et al. (1977), Jarial (1981), Mishra (1982), Dey (1984), Esquivel (1968) and Bawa et al. (1995). Torrance (1959) obtained the coefficients of correlation between divergent thinking and academic achievement ranging from 0.37 to 0.53 with a sample of seventy five children from fourth to sixth grade. Cropley (1967) obtained relationship between creativity and school achievement ranging from 0.16 to 0.42 in a study with 320 Canadian children. Sharma (1977) in his study with 400 Indian students found that high creative boys and girls were high in academic achievement than low creative boys and girls respectively. Singh et al. (1977) found significant correlation between creativity and achievement. Jarial (1981) in his study with 200 Indian students of Class IX found that academic achievement was positively and significantly related to verbal and non-verbal creativity scores of the students and arts students scored significantly higher than the science students on verbal and non-verbal creativity tests. Mishra (1982) tried to obtain relationship between locus of control, creativity and achievement of urban, rural and tribal children. He found the correlation between locus of control and creativity, locus of control and educational achievement, and creativity and educational achievement were positive and highly significant. Dey (1984) in his study with National Rural Talent (NRT) scholarship awardees found that creativity was related to the subsequent school achievement of the NRTs holders.

Esquivel (1988) observed a significant positive relationship between creativity and reading achievement of 160 sifted minority children in grades 1-8. Bawa et al. (1995) in their study with 600 Indian students of Higher Secondary Schools found that there was a strong association between scores on creativity and academic achievement for both male and female students, and creativity and academic achievement in languages end to be better correlated than creativity and achievement in social studies and general science.

The findings of the present study concerning the relationship between academic achievement and different measures of creativity clearly show that verbal fluency measure has stronger association (r ranging from 0.40 to 0.47) with academic achievement in comparison to other measures of creativity. Accordingly the interpretation is that students high in academic achievement are not consistently high scorers on all measures of creativity but they tend to be mentally fluent in using language. It means that the students in this study were apparently able to produce different ideas (mainly verbal), even though many of them were not of different kinds and unique in consideration. The ability to produce large number of ideas verbally seems to be an essential quality for achieving high score in academic subjects. In achievement tests most of the items are usually given in verbal form and the students are required to generate number of ideas for arriving at the solution. Though the students' previous learning experiences etc. of course, play a vital role in this context, the production of sufficient number of ideas towards solution of a particular problem appears most important rather than production of unique or novel ideas because such ideas may not work effectively in achievement tests which are loaded with convergent type items. This observation is in keeping with earlier studies made by Kanderian (1970) and Sawyers (1989). Kanderian (1970) in a study with 400 sixth grade learners in Iraq found that fourth test (i.e. fluency test) of the Guilford's test of creativity showed highest correlation with school achievement. Sawyers (1981) in a study with 81 college students reported that ideational fluency is a valid predictor of sudent achievement in an interior design course.

The findings of the present study concerning the relationship of academic achievement with creativity are not in agreement with the findings of Goyel (1969), Badrinath and Satyanarayanan(1979), and Starr and Nicholl (1975). Goyel (1969) found no relationship of creativity with brightness in academic achievement. Badrinath and Satyanarayanan (1979) in a study with 114 class IX students of five Central schools of the city of Bangalore, found no significant difference in the creativity scores of the students of low, middle and high academic achievement groups. In starr and Nicholl (1975) study with 110 examinees of the Nuffield's ordinary level physics examination, no significant relationship was obtained between creativity and performance in Nuffield's physics examination.

A possible explanation for the disagreement between the findings of the present study and those cited above may be accounted as follows. High correlation between creativity and academic achievement depends on the nature of creativity test used and also the nature of the achievement test taken as the criterion. To expect a significant relationship between creativity and academic achievement both the tests should contain items of divergent types. Lack of presence of divergent type test items may cause low correlation between the two variables. Another cause of the above stated disagreement may be with the difference in the nature of the sample.

(3) One of the objectives of this study was to find the relationship between academic achievement and intelligence primary school children of class IV.

It has been found in the present study that the academic achievement of both boys and girls in Mathematics and Bengali correlated significantly with their intelligence (Tables12, 13, 14 and 15). This has been interpreted by stating that the general intelligence of a student influences his academic achievement. Thus the above findings imply that the students, who are at the low end of intelligence spectrum, are most likely to show poor academic achievement.

The result of the present study is in tune with earlier studies made by Henderson (1964), Downing et al. (1965) and Mac Arthur (1962). Henderson's (1964) study of more than 100 Hong Kong primary school children found a correlation of 0.47 between arithmetic proficiency and intelligence and a correlation of 0.29 between language proficiency and intelligence. Downing et al. (1965) obtained a correlation of 0.56 between the scores on the Metropolitan Reading Test and Cattell's Culture Fair Test of intelligence. Mac Arthur (1962) observed a correlation of 0.46 between f intelligence and California Achievement total score for seventh to ninth graders. The findings of the present study are supported by the study of Cattell and Butcher (1968). In their study the correlation between intelligence and academic achievement (SAT) were found to be 0.54 for urban (N=153) high school children and 0.33 for rural (N=124) high school children. Cattell, Barton and Dielman (1972) examined the relationships among measures of intelligence, achievement test scores and school grades. The results showed that the correlations between intelligence and academic achievement of sixth graders (N-169) in Social Studies, Science, Mathematics and Reading were 0.44, 0.38, 0.60 and 0.52 respectively. For the seventh grade students (N-142) the respective correlations found were 0.47, 0.53, 0.66 and 0.65. Kanderian (1970) also examined the relationships among measures of intelligence and school achievement of 6th grade students in Iraq and found a significant positive correlation (r=0.29).

In India Rajput (1984) studied academic achievement of 435 students of grade V in Mathematics in relation to their intelligence, achievement motivation and socio-economic status. Findings of the study revealed the superiority of high intelligent group of students over average and low intelligent groups of students in their achievement in Mathematics. Roach (1985) found that reading achievement of 6th grade students had significant correlation with their intelligence. Singh (1986) in his study with the students of class XI in India observed a significant relationship between achievement in mathematics and intelligence.

This finding of the present study seems to be quite natural. Students who have obtained high scores on general intelligence test seem to possess the ability to analyse a problem, to find relationships among different components of the problem, to restructure the problem to use suitable abstraction for arriving at the solution. All these qualities of intelligent students help them to achieve good score in different subjects. Although, large number of researches has been done both in this country and abroad, the researcher failed to locate any study contradicting the findings of the present study concerning the relationship of academic achievement with general intelligence.

4. This study attempted to investigate the relationship between academic achievement and cognitive style of primary school children of class IV.

It has been found to the present study that academic achievement of both boys and girls in Mathematics and Bengali correlated significantly with their cognitive style (Tables 12, 13, 14 and 15). This result indicates that cognitive style plays a significant role in students' capability of achieving good scores in academic subjects.

The field dependence independence dimension of cognitive style refers to an individual's ability to extract an item perceptually from its complex context or "field' influences. The field independent individual is one who performs well on this task. The field dependent individual, on the other hand, performs the task poorly. Witkin and his associates (1962) viewed field-dependence-independence cognitive style in the form of a continuum rather than as two distinct categories. At the level of intellectual functioning, the field dependent individual is global in his approach and does not differentiate cognitively between experiences. In contrast, the field independent person separates the object from the field and consequently can be more analytic about his experience. The implication of the present finding is that a student with more analytic cognitive style (i.e., field independent) shows better academic achievement, while a student maintaining a simple and global cognitive style (i.e. field dependent) shows comparatively poor academic achievement. This is because field independent cognitive style helps s the students to recognise relevant attributes of a problem for establishing meaningful relation among them with a view to generate a well organized intellectual move towards the solution of the problem. Thus, the findings of the present study demonstrate that relatively analytic students, who were aware of their senses and felt as if they could use them to aid in solving new problems, tended to actually know what problem solving strategies worked well for them and performed well on tasks of academic achievement tests.

The findings of the present study concerning the relationship between academic achievement and cognitive style are similar to the findings of Bracht and Hopkins (1972), and Testu (1985). Bracht and Hopkins (1972) in their longitudinal studies concluded hat students who are not encouraged to do develop individual style achieve less than those who are encouraged through a system of identification and reinforcement. Testu (1985) found that field independent students performed better than field dependent students on the visual-spatial and mathematics tasks. This study also finds indirect support from the study of Gayatri (1983) in India. Gayatri (1983) found that students with field dependent cognitive style expressed need for continual feedback, structured course work and organized activity. The field independent students, on the other hand, endorsed an exploratory orientation, preferring to work independently and with less structure in their environment.

(5) The present study also attempted to investigate the nature of relationship among variables like creativity, intelligence and cognitive style. The study was concerned with the assumption that the causes behind student's academic achievement are multiple, interdependent and interactive and hence the variables can be best studied in the context of the relationship among the predictor variables. Thus, the relationships among the variables

like creativity, intelligence and cognitive style are important to understand the nature of academic achievement of primary school children.

It has been found from Tables 16 and 17 that

(a) the relationships among different measures of creativity of both boys and girls are positive and significant. The positive and significant associations among different measures of creativity indicate that students who are high on one measure tend to be high on other measures of creativity. This finding finds support from the studies of Torrance (1974) and Raina (1986).

(b) the relationship between intelligence and different measures of creativity of both boys and girls and positive and significant except verbal originality of girls, with which the relationship is positive but non-significant. It means that students who have better score on intelligence tend to have better score on creativity. The researcher is not intended to include here that high intelligence is a precondition to become high creative because students, who are both highly creative and highly intelligent are not often found in the normal classroom. But the present finding concerning association between intelligence and creativity clearly demonstrates that intelligence serves as the base for becoming creative. This observation is in tune with the theory of creativity propounded by the cognitive psychologists like Bruner (1963) and Pribram (1964). Moreover, the present finding gets support from the studies of Passi (1972), Singh et al. (1977), Gupta (1979), Jarial (1981) and Dey (1984).

(c) the relationship between cognitive style and different

measures of creativity of both boys and girls are positive and significant except verbal fluency of the girls, with which the relationship is positive but non significant. This means that students who are high on cognitive style (i.e., field independent) tend to be high on creativity and students who are low on cognitive style (i.e., field dependent) tend to be low on creativity. The present finding concerning relationship between cognitive style and creativity is in agreement with the findings of Ohnmacht (1968), Stevens (1970), Ohnmacht and McMorris (1971), Kumar (1978), Deb (1987) and Rastogi(1987).

(d) the relationship between intelligence and cognitive style of both boys and girls are positive and significant. It indicates that more intelligent students tend to be aware of their senses to use them to perceive in an analytical way and less intelligent students tend to perceive globally due to less awareness of their own senses to aid analytical perception. The present finding is in agreement with the findings of Roach (1985) and Testu (1985).

Thus, the observations concerning positive and significant relationships among creativity, intelligence and cognitive style, demonstrate that in the present study students who were analytic in perception had intelligent ideas and those ideas were sometimes unique and often many in numbers than those students who were global in perception.

(6) In this study academic achievement in Mathematics and Bengali were taken as criterion variables and creativity, intelligence and cognitive style as predictor

variables. One of the objectives of the present study was to investigate the contribution made by the predictor variables jointly towards variance of the criterion variables on one hand and also to examine the relative strength of individual predictor, on the other hand, in predicting the criterion variables.

(a) It has been found from Tables 18 and 21 that multiple correlation (R) between academic achievement of the boys in Mathematics and the predictor variables, like measures of creativity, intelligence and cognitive style is 0.61 ($p < .01$), and multiple correlation (R) between academic achievement of the boys in Bengali and the said predictor variables is 0.64 ($p < .01$). It means that the correlation between the predicted scores in Mathematics from the multiple regression equation and the earned scores in Mathematics of 308 boys will be 0.61. Similarly the correlation between the predicted and earned scores of 308 boys in Bengali will be 0.64. Consequently it implies that the predictor variables jointly explained 37% of variance of achievement in Mathematics (R^2=0.37, $p < .00$) and 41% of variance of achievement in Bengali (R^2 =0.41, $p < .00$). Thus the predictor variables like measures of creativity, intelligence and cognitive style combined together formed a good predictor formula in the form of multiple regression equation for the criterion variables, viz., academic achievement in Mathematics and Bengali of the boys.

Again it has been found from Tables 20 and 23 that three measures were the best predictors and that all contributed statistically to the variance of achievement in both the subjects, i.e., Mathematics and Bengali of the boys. Two of the measures, intelligence and verbal fluency, had positive parameter estimate. The third measure, verbal originality, had a negative parameter estimate. The finding that intelligence and verbal fluency contributed statistically is in keeping with the earlier studies of Kanderian (1970), Rajput (12984), Singh (1986), Sawyers and Canestaro (1989).

The gathering of informational patterns of little children is usually contained in verbal comprehension units. If one knows the meaning of a word, he can learn to see the meaning in groups of words. For example, a child must understand the concept 'tree' to learn the meaning 'a group of trees is forest'. In this way intelligent children can conceptualise the commonalities among the attributes of a group of ideas and can identify the relationships among these ideas. They have general reasoning ability to see the basic relationships in a problem. In achievement tests the students are required to discover an idea which subsumes several given ideas. A student usually sorts ideas into meaningful classes and produces an idea, which is related to another in a specified way. For example, all usually tall, woody plants which have a single trunk are 'trees'. Semantic patterning then allows one to generate a system from several ideas. A palm-tree is usually tall, woody plant which has a single trunk. A coconut tree is usually tall woody plant which has a single trunk. Thus palm. coconut, pine etc. are trees. One may also redefine the semantics one uses and thereby produce a change of interpretation or emphasis of ideas; for example, all usually short, non-woody plants which have single trunk are bushes, not trees. This is also true for mathematical operations also. Mainka (1983) holds that mathematical concepts developed better with pupils good in language and did not develop to their fullest form with poor language. Primary school children generally think and organize mathematical concepts in terms of language. They have to evaluate the words in the mathematical problem to determine which operation(s) to carry out. This activation depends on the associations linking various bits of knowledge together for example, decision about why to use an operation and what different steps in the operation mean, will lead to construction of a larger network of knowledge. This network is richer in conceptual understanding and contains a greater number of concepts and procedures. Thus, intelligence of a student allows him to deduce a statement of results from a set of ideas. For this reason intelligent students usually do well in achievement tests and possibly for the same reason intelligence measure of the boys in the present study emerged as an important predictor of their achievement in Mathematics and Bengali.

That verbal fluency measure emerged as a prominent predictor of achievement in Mathematics and Bengali is important because Fluency Tests call upon the examinee to bring forth from his memory storage as many selected items of information as he can in a short time. In fact verbal fluency involves rapid recall of members of a class of items of information. It may be assumed that each item to be produced has its own level of difficulty. So in case of a verbally fluent student the frequency distribution of such items of a difficulty continuum is likely to be positively skewed, with a relatively large number of items being easy to revive almost immediately and a smaller number spread out towards the most difficult levels. For success in achievement tests, supply of information and ideas at large scale in a short time are essential in making appropriate association of stored information/ideas with the new information to arrive at the result. As verbally fluent students have the advantage in this respect, they seem to do well in achievement tests. In fact the primary school students get ample opportunity to become verbally fluent due to the fact that they are mostly treated in terms of verbal language to think and understand different information in actual classroom situation and verbal language becomes the strongest medium of their thought process, and they used to use their verbal fluency in solving various problems. This may possibly be the reason of emerging verbal fluency as prominent predictor of achievement of the boys in Mathematics and Bengali.

The finding that verbal originality obtained a negative parameter estimate may be interpreted in the following way. The achievement tests contain items mostly in verbal terms, having predetermined correct solution, i.e., they are mostly of convergent type, Naturally the uncommon and unique responses, if generated by the students, hardly get rewarded in such tests,. Another way to account for negative parameter estimate is that this variable (verbal originality) may serve as a moderator variable. Zedeck (1971) suggests that a moderator variable affects the nature or degree of association between a criterion variable and given correlate or set of correlates. Thus, verbal originality may serve as a variable that interacts with other two variables to enhance the predictability of achievement of the boys in Mathematics and Bengali.

(b) It has been found from Tables 24 and 27 that multiple correlation (R) between academic achievement of the girls in Mathematics and the predictor variables like measures of creativity, intelligence and cognitive style is 0.51 ($p < .01$), and multiple correlation (R) between academic achievement of the girls in Bengali and the said predictor variables is 0.52 ($p < .01$). It means that the correlation between the predicted sores in

Mathematics of 197girls will be 0.51. Similarly the correlation between the predicted and earned sores of 197 girls in Bengali will be 0.52. Consequently it implied that the predictor variables jointly explained 26% of variance of achievement in Mathematics ($R^2 = 0.27$, $p <.00$) and 27% of variance of achievement in Bengali ($R^2 = 0.27$, $p <.00$). Thus, the predictor variables like measures of creativity, intelligence and cognitive style combined together formed a good predictor formula for both the criterion variables like academic achievement in Mathematics and Bengali of the girls.

Again it has been found from Tables 26 and 29 that verbal fluency, figural flexibility and intelligence measures of the girls contributed statistically as best predictors to the variance of their achievement in Mathematics, and that verbal fluency, figural elaboration and figural originality measures of the girls contributed statistically as best predictors to the variance of their achievement in Bengali.

The finding that verbal fluency and intelligence measures emerged as prominent predictors of achievement of girls in Mathematics is similar to that of the boys. The possible reasons behind the findings have already been stated. But the emergence of figural flexibility measure of the girls as a prominent predictor of their achievement in Mathematics is an important feature. In fact, most of the problems of achievement test in Mathematics are usually given in a concealed way. To solve such problems the students are often required to produce figural transformation. The transformation required may be in the form of redefinition or reinterpretation of different function or operations known previously to overcome the rigidity of functional fixedness. In this context the observation of Bond (1955) is important. Bond found that it is only necessary for students to observe unusual uses of previously learned strategies (or an object) to prevent the functional fixedness type of response. Since flexibility is conceived as a facility in shifting from one class to another class, students having this ability can readily make transformation in their traditional or fixed strategies to employ them effectively in solving problems of Mathematics. This may possibly be the reason of emerging figural flexibility measure of the girls as an important predictor of their achievement in Mathematics.

The finding that verbal fluency measure emerged as an important predictor of achievement of the girls in Bengali is similar to that of the boys. The causes behind such finding have already been discussed previously. But the emergence of figural elaboration and figural originality as prominent predictors of achievement in Bengali of the girls is interesting. Roe (1951) offered the hypothesis that the type of thinking to which an individual is most accustomed helps to determine one's choice of field. Hedamard (1945) hold that the personal choice may have some relation to the kind of content factors (of 59 model) in which the individual has found he can do his thinking most readily. He may then translate the final product into the language in which he finally intend to communicate to others. In the present study, the girls seem to have efficiency in communicating their figural thinking through language. Elaboration refers to the different ideas used to build or construct the particular idea or picture, that is, elaboration of the basic idea by the addition of supporting ideas. It indicates an individual's ability to implement and build his 'big idea' on the basic idea by adding other ideas to it. Torrance (1969) hold that an individual who operates on a relatively high level of differentiation and integration is able to conceive and draw complex ideas. Girls of Indian society are often found to have a tendency in making different pictures interesting by elaborating the main ideas relating to floor decoration (alpana), ornamentation of human figures, drawings from nature like plant forms, flower forms, still-life study etc. They are habituated to think in terms of figures for differentiating and integrating different ideas to the main idea. Such ability of figural elaboration may also facilitate their thinking even in elaborating a basic idea supplied in verbal forms. In achievement test in Bengali verbal items relating to cause-effect relationship between ideas and events, locating of main ideas of a text, finding of consequences of any event in a written text etc. require elaboration of the main ideas for their solutions. Thus the girls of the present study, having such facility seem to do well in this context and for this reason figural elaboration possibly emerged as a prominent predictor of their achievement in Bengali.

Originality means generating novel responses which are rare and unusual because they are remotely associated with the stimulus. The obvious responses are more direct and almost anyone would think of them. For securing good sore in achievement test, production of remote responses is often required in addition to the production of obvious responses. Remote responses are distant in a chain of events or pertain to some often over-looked aspects of the problems. The girls in the present study, having the facility of figural thinking in an unusual way seem to apply this mental trait to identify the often overlooked aspect or the chain of events of the verbal problems of achievement test in Bengali rather readily. For this reason figural originality perhaps emerged as an important predictor of achievement in Bengali of the girls.

Conclusion of the Study

On the basis of the discussion made above the following conclusions may be drawn as the outcome of the present study:

(1) That the performance of the boys is better than that of the girls on all measures of creativity, intelligence and cognitive style.

(2) That academic achievement of the boys (in Mathematics as well as in Bengali) has positive relationship with different measures of their creative thinking ability, their intelligence and their cognitive style.

(3) That academic achievement of the girls)in Mathematics as well as in Bengali) has positive relationship with different measures of their creative thinking ability, their intelligence and their cognitive style.

(4) That the measures of creative thinking ability, intelligence and cognitive style of the boys combined together is a good predictor of their academic achievement (in both Mathematics and Bengali).

(5) That the measures of creative thinking ability, intelligence and cognitive style of the girls combined together is a good predictor of their academic achievement (in both Mathematics and Bengali).

(6) That verbal fluency and intelligence of the primary school children have relatively strong impact on their academic achievement. But accountable

contributions of some other predictor variables like verbal originality, figural flexibility, figural originality and figural elaboration are also found in different occasions. However, it can be said that the mutual interactions of all the predictor variables of the present study seem to enhance the predictability of academic achievement of primary school children, although all of them have not emerged as significant predictors in every occasion.

The overall findings of the present study suggest that primary school students need at least average intelligence to be successful in academic achievement. If moderate or average intelligence is supplemented with analytic awareness and creativity, the students stand a good chance at being successful in academic achievement.

Implications of the Study

The gender difference with respect to different cognitive variables like creative thinking ability, Intelligence and Cognitive Style favouring boys, as the result of this study indicated, highlighted the hard spots of child-rearing practices prevailing in Indian society. Analysis of the existing social conditions, though not the purpose of this study, provides realistic perspective to the findings as far as this study is concerned. It has been discovered that less creative students are subject to authoritarian child-raring practices (Nichols, 1964) and high levels of parental control and lower levels of autonomy than their more effective counterparts (Datta and Perlof, 1967). The parental encouragement, freedom, warmth, flexibility and tolerance for their children irrespective of their sex help them to perform better in intellectual activities. Girls of Indian society do not usually enjoy these parental stimulations equally with their ale counterparts. Because of some long prevailing social and cultural taboos, the parents are afraid of allowing that much individual freedom to their daughters as is usually allowed to their sons. If the most desirable values characterizing girls tend to be accepted as meekness, being well-behaved, working soft and so on, the girls will automatically learn to adjust through conformity. Some would rather underachieve and be popular than achieve honour, status and risk of social ostracism.

On the basis of the present findings the researcher is in the opinion that the parents and teachers must check this social calamity with full force and real commitment, and for this they must develop competencies to accept and reward the talents of the girls equally with the boys at home, school and society. They can at best serve as role models through their own achievement orientation and intellectual pursuit while creating an enriched educational environment inside and outside of the school and urging the children, specially the girls, to advance their studies to the fullest extent. They must create democratic set up and encourage the young children to become free, self expressive, curious and inventive and the like. They should provide a variety of learning materials suited to the varied interests of the children and encourage them with equal emphasis for both the sexes to learn at home and in school. These approached will help the parents and teachers to receive social recognition and support from all levels for removing disparity of childrearing practices of Indian society.

The relationships of academic achievement with creativity, intelligences and cognitive style of primary school children, as revealed from the present study, illuminated the need of taking some steps that would give the student a chance of independent and imaginative exploration, interpreting different events without ridicule and perceiving things in the ways he does, according to his own intellectual/cognitive style. But it has been noticed that vast majority of students are not exposed to challenges which would be their potential for independent thinking, innovations, etc. because the whole system of primary education particularly in India is characterized by rote learning and repetitive exercises. In order to allow free and independent cognitive functioning of primary school children, following changes are recommended. It is not only traditional learning which needs to be stressed; instead free thinking should receive relatively greater attention as an objective of education. This change in objective should be associated with innovative methods of teaching, curriculum renewal, improvised instructional material, effective use of learning time and positive attitude of the teaching personnel.

The role of teachers in this context becomes very important in freeing his students to function at their ma^imum capacity. The present study clearly demonstrates that in classroom instruction, if the overall quality of student work is to improve, there is a need to utilize the traits of intelligence, creative thinking ability and cognitive style of the students. For this purpose, in the opinion of the present researcher on the basis of the findings of his study, a classroom teacher may discharge his duties at three different levels. At the first level, the teacher ay explain in detail the content of specific subject and familiarize the students with the fundamental or basic thinking skills for analyzing and then generating ideas. These basic thinking skills include both convergent or analytical thinking technique (such as making inferences and deducing, using evidence, categorizing, et.) and divergent or creative thinking techniques (such as syntactic, role-playing, brainstorming, cubing, mapping, free-writing, free-drawing, group discussion etc.). Of course, by teaching about both kinds of thinking, the teacher may succeed in giving the students a chance to feel positive about their unique abilities. In this stage the teacher's role is two-fold; facilitator of learning and dispenser of information.

At the second level, the teacher should move away from teaching about thinking skills and move into emphasis on leading students in their efforts to master and apply problem solving methods to various assignments given to them. He must encourage students to ask question and guess consequences about the problems, and allow them to find unifying principles which demonstrate the relatedness of segments of knowledge apparently held separate. He needs to encourage them to recognize the existence of and seek alternative solutions to the problem. He should accept all sorts of ideas put forward by the little student even when they are apparently contrary to established principles so that the student may understand that the teacher is glad to have his ideas and welcomes it with pleasure. In other words, the emphasis should be on the production of ideas rate than merely of correct solutions. He then criticizes ineffective and non-relevant productions to let the student deduce his own shortcomings rather than bringing them directly to his notice. But criticisms should always be associated with strong expressions of approval so that the criticism is not seen as a rejection of the proposal put forward by the student. If the student is still unable to see any way in which the solution offered can be improved, the teacher may draw the attention of all students in a group to discuss and debate over the issue to generate appropriate solution. In watching the teacher taking part with the students in this process of learning, the students come to know that learning to solve problems is more than following a generic recipe and it is sort of challenging interactive puzzle instead of a boring formula. In short, the teacher at this level leads them to understand that learning and solving problem is a dynamic process, not a static one.

At the third level the students are challenged to use the basic thinking skills ad the problem solving methods that they have learned to deal with a real problem. The transfer of learning from level 1 and level 2 may not automatically occur at the third level. The teacher is, thus, supposed to be very careful to provide explicit activities and experiences that will promote application and transfer of learning. In this context observation made by Torrance is important. Torrance (1984) has indicated that mentorship experiences (or the lack of them) have potent effects on creative productivity.

Besides classroom teaching there are numerous activities which can be organized in the primary schools. Of these the useful ones may be exhibitions on various subjects, devising of indigenous apparatus, extempore debates, quiz programmers etc. Situational talks and small-size special or extra classes in which practice may be given in 'brain-storming', 'deferred judgment' and other similar techniques aimed at improving thinking pier of students without any fixed curriculum. Other activities may include music, dance, drama, drawing, clay modeling, games and athletics etc. All these activities are to be organized in primary schools in such a way as to give direct benefit to the students in their curricular subjects which happen to be the ultimate points for consideration for an examination as well as career.

Another important area is examination and evaluation. As the way of teaching primary school students is to be hanged the examination and evaluation system at the primary state is also to be revised to the extent that flexibility of idea, uniqueness, originality, fluency and divergent products are given due weight age. To translate it into practice it would be necessary to devise and popularize new tests in various school subjects which may be capable of bringing into play such abilities as stated below. The prevailing written and oral examinations may also be modified so as to give these abilities a fair chance for assessment.

It should be made clear that the researcher is not intended to say that every student in every classroom should be treated to make a creative genius. As all children are capable of asking and wondering, of guessing and supposing, of questioning and speculating, a school which fosters creativity, analytical thinking and independent awareness, facilitates learning in all children. In case of a student with marked creative potential a relativity centred classroom will help to develop his creative talents to the full while, in the case of the non-creative, approaching knowledge through creativity will help him to understand the way in which knowledge is organized, and will make him more efficient finder of solutions.

Bibliography

Acharyulu, S.T.V.G. (1978). A Study of the Relationship among Creative Thinking, Intelligence and School Achievement; Doctoral Thesis, Utkal University.

Adler, A. (1927). *The Practice and Theory of Individual Psychology;* New York: Harcourt Brace.

Amabile, T.M. (1983). *The Social Psychology of Creativity;* New York: Springer-Verlag.

American Educational Research Association (1955). *Technical Recommendations for Achievement Test;* Washington D.C: Author.

Anastasi, A. (1982). *Psychological Testing* (5th Ed); New York: Macmillan Publishing Company.

Anderson, H.H. (Ed.) (1959). *Creativity and its Cultivation.* New York : Harper & Row.

Anderson, J.E. (1976). The Nature of Abilities, In E.P. Torrance (Ed.). *Talent and Education;* Minnepolis : University of Minnesota Press.

Antonak, R.F. (1988). Relationships Between Group 10 and Scholastic Achievement At Grades Two, Four and Six; *Annual Psychological Abstract,* 77, 08642.

Ault, R.L., Crawford, D.E., and Jeffry, W.E. (1972). Visual scanning Strategies of Reflective, Impulsive, Fast accurate, and Slow inaccurate children on the Matching Familiar Fig. Test; *Child Development,* 43, 1412-17.

Badrinath, S. and Satyanarayan, S.B. (1979). Correlates of Creative Thinking of High School Students; *Creativity Newsletter,* Vol. 7 & 8, No. 2 & 1.

Barron, F. (1968). *Creativity and Personal Freedom.* Princeton, N.J : Van Nostrand.

Barron, F. (1969). *Creative Person and Creative Process;* New York: Holt, Rinehart and Winston.

Barron, F. and Harrington, D. M. (1981). Creativity, Intelligence, and Personality; *Annual Review of Psychology,* 32, 439-476.

Basu, N.M. and Jawa, P. (1973). Personality Composition of the Artists; *Indian Journal of Psychology,* 35.

Bawa, S.K. and Kaur, P. (1995). Creativity and Academic Achievement ; *Psycho-Lingua,* 25 (1& 2), 133-136.

Beeby, C.E. (1966) . *The Quality of Education in Developing Countries;* Cambridge, Mass.: Harvard University Press.

Benavot, A. and Kamens, D. (1989). The curricular content of Primary Education in Developing Countries. Policy, Planning and Research Working Paper; World Bank, Population and Human Resource Department, Washington D.C.

Bennett, D.H. (1956). Perception of the upright in relation to body image; *The Journal of Mental Science*. 102, 487-506.

Berk, R.A. (Ed.) (1984). *A Guide to Criterion-Referenced Test Construction*. Baltimore, Md.: John Hopkins University Press.

Berlyne, D.E. (1965). *Structure and Direction in Thinking*. London: John Wiley.

Bloom, B. (1985). *Developing Talent in Young Children*. New York: Ballantine.

Berry, J. W. (1979), Culture and Cognitive Style; In A. Marsella, R. Tharp and T. Ciborowski (Eds.), *Perspectives on Cross-Cultural Psychology*, New York: Academic Press.

Berry, J. (1991). Cultural Variation in Field Dependence-Independence, In S. Wapner and J. Demick (Eds), *Field Dependence–Independence Cognition Style Across the life span*; Hillsdale, N.J.: Erlbaum.

Best, J. W. and Kahn, J.V. (1995). *Research in Education* (Seventh Edition); New Delhi. Prentice Hall of India Pvt. Ltd.

Bloom, B. S, Krathwohl, D.R, Masia, B.B. (1964). *Taxonomy of Educational Objectives*; Michigan: David McKay Company.

Bloom, B. (1982). *Human Characteristics and School Learning*; NY: McGraw Hill.

Bloomberg, M. (1971). Creativity as Related to Field-Independence and Mobility, *Journal of Genetic Psychology*, 118, 3-12.

Bond, N.A. (1955). An Experimental Study of Transfer Effects in Human Problem Solving; Unpublished Doctoral Dissertation, University of Southern California.

Bolton, N. (1972). *The Psychology of Thinking*. London: Methuen.

Bracht, G.H. and Hopkins, K.D. (1972). Stability of Educational Achievement; In *Perspectives in Education and Psychological Measurement*. Englewood : Prentice Hall.

Bruner, J.S. and Olver, R.R. (1962). Basic Cognition Processes in Children; *Child Development Monograph*, No. 86, 28.

Bethel, D.M. (Ed). (1989). *Education for Creative Living, Ideas and Proposals of Tsunesabura Makiguchi;* Ames: Iowa State University Press.

Cahan, S. and Ganor, Y. (1995). Cognitive gender differences among Israeli children; *Sex Roles: A Journal of Research*, Vol. 32, 1995.

Cattell, R.B. , (1966). *Hand Book of Multivariate Experimental Psychology;* Chicago: Hand, McNally.

Cattell, R.B., and Butcher, H.J. (1968). *The Prediction of Achievement and Creativity;* New York: Bobbs-Merrill.

Cattell, R.B. (1971). *Abilities Their Structure, Growth and Action;* Boston : Houghton Miffilin.

Cattell, R.B., Barton, K. and Dielman, T.E. (1972). Personality, Motivation and IQ Measures as Predictors of School Achievement; *Journal of Educational Psychology*. 63, 4, 398-404.

Cattell, R.B. (1973). *Culture Fair Tests of Intelligence and Manual; Scale* 2. Illinois : Institute of Personality and Ability Testing.

Chadha, N.K. (1985). Creativity and Cognitive Style; *Psycho-Lingua*, 15(2), 81-88.

Chall, Jeanne S. (1983). *Stages of Reading Development;* New York : McGraw-Hill.

Chapman , D.W. and Carol , A.C. (ed). (1990). *Improving Educational Quality: A Global Prospective;* West Port, Conn. : Greenwood Press.

Chase, C. (1984). Review of the Torrance Tests of Creative Thinking; *Buras Mental Measurement Year book*, 9th Edition.

Cline, V.R., Richards, J.M. and Needham, W.E. (1963). Creativity Tests and Achievement in High School science; *Journal of Applied Psychology.* 47, 184-189.

Coachren, S.H. (1979). *Fertility and Education : What Do We Really Know?* Johns Hopkins University Press, Baltimore.

Cohen, J., and Cohen, P. (1983). *Applied Multiple Regression/ Correlation Analysis for The Behavioural Sciences* (Second Edition); New Jersey : Lawrence Erlbaum Associates Publishers.

Cohen, A. and Hale, H. (1974). Conceptual Styles, Culture, Conflict and Non Verbal Tests of Intelligence; *American Anthropologist,* 71, 828-856.

Comean, H. (1980). The Relationship between Sex, Birth Order and Creativity; *Journal of Creative Behaviour,* 14, 1, 71.

Coop, A. H. and Sigel, L.E. (1971). Cognitive Style: Implications for Learning and Instruction; *Psychology in the Schools* 2, 152-161.

Counts, P.D. (1972), A Study of Relationship between Academic Achievement and Creativity; *Dissertation Abstracts International,* 32 (8-A), 4342.

Crawford, R.P. (1954). *Techniques of Creative Thinking;* New York: Hawthorne Books.

Cropley, A.J. (1966) . Creativity and Intelligence; *British Journal of Educational Psychology,* 36, 259-266.

Cropley , A.J. (1967). *Creativity.* London; Longmans, Green & Co. Ltd.

Cropley, A.J. (1967). Creativity, Intelligence and Achievement; *Ait. Journal of Educational Research.*

Cummings, W.K. (1986). *Low-cost Primary Education: Implementing an Innovation in Six Nations;* Ottawa, Ontario : International Development Research Centre.

Cureton, E.E. (1951). Validity in E.F. Lindquist (Ed.), *Educational Measurement;* Washington D.C.

Dalbect, E. (1966). Creative Development over a Three-Year Period in a Catholic Liberal Arts College. Master's Thesis, University of Minnesota, Minneapolis.

Datta, L.E. and Perloff (1967). On the Relevance of Autonomy : Parent-Child Relationships and Early Scientific Creativity; *Proceedings of the Seventy-fifth Annual Convention of the American Psychological Association,* Washington D.C.

Dave. P.N. et al. (1988). Pupil Achievement at The Primary Stage; *Fourth Survey of Research in Education,* N.C.E.R.T., New Delhi, 1266.

Dawson, J.L.M. (1967). Cultural and Physiological Influence upon Spatial Perceptual Processes in West Africa; Part I & II. *International Journal of Psychology,* 2, 115-218 and 171-185.

De, B. (1985), Cognitive Style and Cognitive Ability of Tribal and non Tribal School Pupils; *Fourth Survey of Research in Education,* N.C.E.R.T. New Delhi, 351.

Deehan, R.J. and Havighurst, R.J. (1961). Educating Gifted Children; Chicago : The University of Chicago Press.

Dey, B. (1984). The relationship of Creativity to Intelligence and Academic Achievement of National Rural Talent Scholarship Awardees; Doctoral Thesis, Utkal University.

Deutsch, U. et. Al. (1967). *The Disadvantaged Child: Studies of the Social Environment and the Learning Process;* New York : Basic Books.

Directorate of Primary Education, Govt. of West Bengal (1979). Prathamik Sikshar Sikshakram of Pathyasuchi (Curriculum and Syllabi of Primary Education) Calcutta : Author.

Dixit , M.K. (1985) A Comparative Study of Intelligence and Academic Achievement of Adolescent Boys and Girls Studying in Classes IX and XI ; Doctoral Thesis, Kanpur University.

Dossey, J. A. Mullis, I.V. Lindquist. M.M. and Chambers, D.L. (1983). The Mathematics Card : Are we Measuring Up? *National Assessment for Educational Process.* Educational Testing Service, Princeton , N. J.

Downing , G. L. Edgar., R.W., Harris, A.J., Kornberg, L. and Storen, H.F. (1965). *The Preparation of Teachers for School in Culturally Deprived Neighbourhoods;* Queens College of the City University of New York.

Dark, D.M. (1970). Perceptual Correlates of Impulsive and Reflective Behaviour Developmental; *Psychology.* 2, 202-14.

Dunn, R., and Dunn, K. (1974). *Learning styles as a Criterion for Placement in Alternative Programmes;* Phi Delta Kappa, Dec; 275-278.

Dyk, R.B. (1969). An Exploratory study of Mother – Child Interaction in Infancy as Related to the Development of Differentiation. *Journal of the American Academy of Child Psychiatry,* 8,657-691.

Ebel, R.L.(1966). *Measurement in Educational Measurement;* New Delhi : Prentice Hall of India Pvt. Ltd.

Erikson, E.H. (1963). *Childhood and Society* (2nd ed.). New York: W.W. Norton.

Esquivel , G.B. and Lopez , E (1988). Correlations Among Measures of Cognitive Ability, Creativity and Academic Achievement for Gifted Minority Children; *Annual Psychological Abstract,* 76, 25449.

Feldhusen, J. and Clinkenbeard, P. (1986). Creativity Instructional Materials: A Review of Research; *Journal of Creative Behaviour,* 20.

Ferguson, G.A. (1981). *Statistical Analysis in Psychology and Education* (5th ed .); New York : Mc Graw-Hill.

Freeman, F.S. (1965). *Theory and Practice of Psychological Testing.* New Delhi: Oxford and IBH Publishing Company Pvt. Ltd.

Forst, J.l. and Hawkes , G.R. (1966). *The Disadvantaged Child: Issues and Innovations;* Boston : Houghton Mifflin Company.

Freud, S. (1958). *On Creativity and Unconscious;* N.Y.; Harper.

Gagneja, S.C. (1972). A Study of Creativity in ninth class Students in Relation to Sex, Residential Background, academic Achievement and Parental Occupation; Master's Thesis, Punjabi University.

Garret, H.E. (1981). *Statistics in Psychology and Education;* Bombay : Vakils, Feffer and Simons Ltd.

Gayatri, H.R. (1983) Educational Orientation and Related Factors Effecting the Academic Achievement of University students; Doctoral Thesis, Jawaharlal Nehru University.

Getzels, J.W. and Jackson, P.W. (1962). *Creativity and Intelligence;* New York: Wiley.

Gimeno, J.B. and Ricardo, M.I. (1981). *The Education of Primary and Secondary School Teachers: an International Comparative study;* Paris: UNESCO.

Glass, G.V. and Hopkins, K.D.(1984). *Statstical Methods*

in Education and Psychology (2nd ed.); Englewood Cliffs, NJ: Pentice-Hall.

Goldstein, K. and Blackman, S. (1978) *Cognitive Style;* Wiley: NY.

Gowan, J.C. et al. (1967). Creativity: Its Educational Implications; NY: Wiley.

Goyal, R.P. (1969). A study of some Personality Traits of Creative Children at Middle School Stage; Unpublished Masters' Thesis, University of Aligarh.

Gruber, H.E. and Barret, P.H. (Ed.) (1974). *A Psychological Study of Scientific Creativity;* New York : E.P. Dulton. Published in one volume with Darwin on man.

Guilford, J.P. (1956). Structure of Intellect; *Psychological Bulletin.* 53, 267-293.

Guilford, J.P. (1959). Traits of Creativity. In Anderson. H.H. (Ed.); *Creativity and its Cultivation.* New York: Harper and Row.

Guilford, J.P. (1967). *The Nature of Human Intelligence;* New York: McGraw-Hill.

Guilford, J.P. (1971). *Psychometric Methods* (Second Edition); New Delhi : Tata Mcgraw-Hill Publishing Co. Ltd.

Gupta, K.K. (1979). Creativity, Intelligence and Achievement; *The Educational Review,* 85(11), 208-212.

Guilford, J.P. and Fruchter, B. (1981). *Fundamental Statistics in Psychology and Education* (Sixth edition) Singpore: McGraw-Hill Book Company.

Guilford, J.P. (1986). *Creative Talents: Their Uses and Development;* Buffalo, N.Y : Bearly Limited.

Hadamard, J.S. (1945). *An Essay on the Psychology of Invention in the Mathematical Field;* Princeton, N.J.: Princeton University Press.

Haddon, F.A. and Lytton H. (1971). Primary Education

and Divergent Thinking Abilities; *British Journal of Educational Psychology,* 41, 136-147.

Henderson, N.K. (1964). The Attainment and Ability of Hong Kong Primary IV Pupils; Hong Kong Council for Educational Research.

Hennessey, Beth A. and Amabile, T.M. (1988). The Conditions of Creativity; In R.J Sternberg (Ed.), *The Nature of Creativity.* Cambridge: Cambridge University Press, 11–38.

Houtz, J. et al. (1983). Predictive Validity of Teacher Ratings of Creativity Over two Years; *Contemporary Educational Psychology,* 8.

Hunt, J. McV. (1961). *Intelligence and Experience;* New York: Ronald Press.

Jarial, G.S. (1981). Creativity. Intelligence and Academic Achievement Their Relationship and Difference with reference to Sex and Academic Subjects; *Journal of Education and Psychology,* 39, 2.

Jimenez, E., Lockheed, M.E., Paqueo, V. (1991). The Relative Efficiency of Private and Public Schools in Developing Countries; World Bank Research Observe, Washington, D.C.

Joseph, C.B. (1966). Creativity and Academic Achievement; *Journal of Educational Research.* 59(6), 269–272.

Jung, Carl G. (1963). Modern Man in Search of a Soul; New York: Harcourt Brace.

Kanderian, S.S. (1970). Study of the Relationship between School Achievement and Measure of Intelligence and Creativity for Students in Iraque; *Dissertation Abstracts International,* 31(2-A), 644.

Karp, S.A. and Konstadt, n. (1971). The Children's Embedded Figures Test and Manual; California : Consulting Psychologists Press.

Kerliger, F.N. and Pedhazur, E.J. (1973). *Multiple Regression in Behavioural Research;* New York : Holt, Rinehart and Winston.

Kato, N. (1965). Creativity School Attitude and Intelligence Relationships in Grade Four, Six and Eight; *Dissertation Abstracts,* 25(11), 6390.

Kim, J. and Michael, W.B. (1995). The Relationship of Creativity Measures to School Achievements and Preferred Learning and Thinking Style in a Sample of Korean High School Students; *Educational and Psychological Measurement,* 55(1), 60-74.

Kirk, R.E. (1982). *Experimental Design: Procedures for the Behavioural Sciences* (2nd Ed.) Belmont, CA : Brooks/ Cole.

Kogan, N. (1976). Cognitive styles in Infancy and Early Childhood; N.Y: Wiley.

Kohler, W. (1969). The Task of Gestalt Psychology; Princeton: Princeton University Press.

Krop, M. (1969) Effects of Extrinsic Motivation, Intrinsic Motivation, and Intelligence on Creativity: A Factorial Approach; *Journal of General Psychology,* 80, 259-266.

Kumar, G. (1978). Creativity in Relation to Cognitive Style, Risk-Taking and Personality; Unpublished Doctoral Thesis, Meerut University.

Leedy, M.G; Lalonde, D. and Runk, K. (2003) Gender Equity in Mathematics: Beliefs of Students, Parents, and Teachers; *School Science and Mathematics,* Vol. 103.

Lindquist, E.F. (1942). *A First Course in Statistics* (Ref. Ed.). Boston : Houghton Miffilin Company.

Lockheed, M.E.; Verspoor, A.M. et al. (1991). *Improving Primary Education in Developing Countries.* Oxford University Press.

Lockheed, M.E.; Jamison, D.T. and Law, L. (1980). Farmer Education and Form Efficiency: A Survey; *Economic Development and Cultural Change*, 29(1), 37-76.

MacArthur, R.S. (1962). Assessing the Intellectual Ability of Indian and Metis Pupils at Fort Simpson, N.W.T; Department of Northern Affairs and Natural Resources.

MacKinnon, D.W. (1963). Identifying and Developing Creativity; *Journal of Secondary Education*, 38, 166-174.

Mahler, M., Pine, F. and Bergman, A. (1975). *The Psychological Birth of the Human Infant;* New York: Basic Books.

Mehta, A.C. (2004). *Elementary Education in India: Where Do We Stand?;* New Delhi: National Institute of Educational Planning and Administration.

Mainka, G.K. (1983). Acquisition of Concept in Mathematics of Pupils at Primary School Level, and its Relation to Some Personal and Environmental Variable of the Pupils; Doctoral Thesis, Bombay University.

Mar'I S.K. (1976). Toward a Cross-Cultural Theory of Creativity; *The Journal of Creative Behaviour*, 66, 2, 108.

Mansfield, R.S. and Busse, T.V (1980). Theories of Creativity; *Journa' of Creativity Behaviour*, 14, 2, 91-103.

Mansfield, R.S. and Busse, T.V (14981). *The Psychology of Creativity and Discovery;* Chicago : Nelson-Hall.

Marshall, S.P. and Smith, J.D. (1987). Sex Difference in Learning Mathematics : A Longitudinal Study with Item and Error Analyses; *The Journal of Educational Psychology*, 79(4).

Marx, A.H (Ed.) (1969). *Learning Process;* London : Collier-Macmillan.

Maslow, A.H. (1958). Emotional Blocks to Creativity; *Journal of Individual Psychology,* 14, 51-56.

Maslow, A.H (1962). *Towards a Psychology of Being;* Princeton, N.J. : D. Van Nostrand.

Matsumoto, A.R.; Fan, X and Chen, M. (1997). Gender Differences in Mathematics Achievement: Findings from the National Education Longitudinal Study of 1988; *Journal of Experimental Education,* Vol. 65.

May, R. (1959). The Nature of Creativity; In J.E. Anderson (Ed.). *Creativity and Its Cultivation.* New York: Harper and Row.

McKinney, J. D (1975). Problem Solving Strategies in Reflective and Impulsive Children; *Journal of Educational Psychology,* 67, 807-20.

Meer, B. and Stein, H.I (1955). Measures of Intelligence and Creativity; *Journal of Psychology,* 39, 117-26.

Mednick, S.A. (1962). The Associative Basis of the Creative Process; *Psychological Review,* 69, 220-232.

Mehdi, B. (1977). Creativity, Intelligence and Achievement-A Correlation Studies; *Psychological Studies,* 22(1), 55-62.

Melton, A.W. (Ed.) (1964). *Categories of Human Learning;* London: Academic Press.

Messick, S. (1976). Personality Consistencies in Cognition and Creativity; In S. Messick and Associates, *Individual in Learning;* San Francisco : Jossey-Bass.

Mishra, C. (1986). Locus of Control, Creativity and Educational Achievement of Urban, Rural and Tribal Children; *Indian Educational Review,* vol. XXI, 4.

Mitra, S.K., Guha Roy, S. and Ray, S.S (1995). *Achievement Level of Primary School Children at the Class IV, Report of a Sample Survey;* Calcutta: Indian Statistical Institute, Calcutta and State Council of Educational Research and Training.

Murphy, G. (1966). What can youth tell us about its potentialities. *National Association of Secondary School Principal's Bulletin,* 310, 20-26.

Nagose, C.K. (1984). A Factorial Study of Divergent Abilities, Aptitudes. Level of Aspirations and Scholastic Achievement; Doctoral Thesis, Nagpur University.

Naik, J.P. (1965). *Elementary Education in India: The Unfinished Business.* New Delhi: Asia Publishing House.

National Policy on Education (1986); New Delhi: Ministry of Human Resource Development, Government of India.

N.C.E.R.T. (1992). *Fifth all India Educational Survey;* vol. I & II. New Delhi: Author.

N.C.E.R.T. (1991). Minimum Levels of Learning at Primary Stage (Report of the Committee set up by the Ministry of Human Resources Development, Govt. of India); New Delhi: Author.

N.C.E.R.T. (1988). *In-Service Teacher Education Package of Primary School Teachers;* New Delhi : Author.

Nicholas, R. (1964). Parental Attitudes of Mothers of Intelligent Adolescents and Creativity of Their Children; *Child Development,* 35, 1041-1049.

Ogletree, E. (1971). A Cross Cultural Examination of the Creative Thinking Ability of Public and Private School Pupils In England, Scotland and Germany; Journal of Social Psychology, 83, 301-302.

Ohnmacht, F.W. (1968). Cognitive Perception and Creativity; *Encyclopedia of Educational Research,* London : Macmillan.

Ohnmacht, F.W. and Mcmorris, J.W. (1971). Creativity and Cognitive Style; *Dissertation Abstract*, 1971.

Okonji, M.O. (1969). The Differential Effects of Rural and Urban Upbringing on The Development of Cognitive Styles; *International Journal of Psychology*, 4, 293-305.

Olive, H. (1972). A Note on Sex Differences In Adolescents' Divergent Thinking. *Journal of Psychology*, 82, 1, 39-42.

Onyejiaku, F. O.(1982).Cognitive Styles, Instructional Strategies, and Academic Performance; *Journal of Experimental Education*, Vol. 51.

Padhi, J.S (1995). Influence of Creativity on Academic Performance; *Journal of Indian Education*, 20(6), 46-51.

Passi, B.K. (1972). An Exploratory Study of Creativity and Its Relationship with Intelligence and Achievement in School Subjects at Higher Secondary Stage; Doctoral Thesis. Pan. University.

Pathak, P. (1962). Experimental Study of Creativity and Intelligence in School Achievement, *Psychological Studies*, 7, 1-9.

Perkins, D. (1981). *The Mind's Best Work*. Cambridge, M.A. : Harvard University Press.

Piaget, J. (1958). *Childhood to Adolescence*; NY : Basic Books.

Piaget, J. (1969). *The Mechanisms of Perception*. New York: Basic Books.

Prakash, A.O. (1966). Understanding the Fourth Grade Slump. A Study of the Creative Thinking of Indian Students; Masters' Thesis, University Of Minnesota.

Pribram, K.H. (1964). Neurological Notes on the Art of Educating. In Hilgard, E.R (Ed.), NSSE Year Book,

LXIII. Chicago University Of Chicago Press.

Prince, G.U. (1970). *The Practice of Creativity.* New York: Harper & Row.

Psacharopoulus, G. (1975). Earning and Education In OECD Countries. Paris : Organisation for Economic Co-Operations and Development.

Psacharopoulus, G. And Maureen, W. (1985). *Education for Development; An Analysis of Investment Choices.* New York : Oxford University Press.

Raina, M.K. (1968). A Study of Some Correlates of Creativity In Indian Students, Ph.D. Thesis, University of Rajasthan.

Raina, M.K. (1969). Sex Differences In Creativity In India; *The Journal of Creative Behaviour,* 3, 111-14.

Raina, M.K. (1970). A Study of Creativity in Teachers; *Psychological Studies,* 15, 38-33.

Raina, M.K (1986). *Talent and Creativity;* New Delhi: N.C.E.R.T.

Rajput, A.S. (1984). Study of Academic Achievement of Students in Mathematics in Relation to Their Intelligence, Achievement Motivation and Socio-Economic Status; Doctoral Thesis, Punjabi University.

Rastogi, M. (1987). A Study of Cognitive Style in Relation to Intelligence and Creativity; *Annual Psychological Abstract,* 75, 29574.

Resnick, Lauren, B. (1987). *Education and Learning to Think;* Washington D.C. : National Press.

Roach, D.A (1985). Effects of Cognitive Style, Intelligence and Sex on Reading Achievement. *Perceptual-and-Motor-Skills,* Vol. 61 (3, Pt. 2), 1139-1142.

Rhodes, M. (1961). An Analysis of Creativity . *Phi Delta Kappa,* 42, 305.

Roe, A. (1951). A Study of Imagery in Research Scientists. *Journal of Personality,* 19, 459-470.

Rogers, C. (1961). *On Becoming a Person.* Boston: Houghton Mifflin.

Rosenthal , A. Et Al. (1983). Comparison of Interpreter Reliability on The TTCT for Gifted and Non-Gifted Students. *Psychology in The Schools,* 20.

Rungsinan , W. (1976). *Scoring of Originality of Creative Thinking Across Cultures.* University of Georgigia.

Ruth, D.C (1976). The Effectiveness of Peer Counselors and Certificated Counselors in the Reducing Student Withdrawals in a Community College; *Dissertation Abstracts International,* 36 (11-A), 7218-19.

Saha, S. (1977). A Study on Relationship between Cognitive Style and Academic Achievement of Elementary School Children; *Journal of Education,* Rabindra Bharati University, Kolkata, II(1), 30-34.

Sawyers, J.K. And Canestaro, N.C (1989). Creativity and Achievement an Design Course Work; *Annual Psychological Abstract,* 78, 02821.

S.C.E.R.T. (1986). *Sikshan Dipika* (Curriculum Guide); Calcutta : Author.

S.C.E.R.T. (1989). *Prathamik Sikshak Sikshan Sahaika* (Primary Teachers' Training Guide); Calcutta: Author.

Schachtel, E.G. (1959). *Metamorphoses;* New York : Basic Books.

Scribner, C.; and Cole, U. (1981). *The Psychology of Literacy;* Cambridge: Harvard University Press.

Sharma, A.K. (1981). Creativity in Relation to Socio-Economic Status and Academic Achievement; *Experiments in Education,* 9, 153.

Sharma, M. (1977). A Study of Some Factors In Relation to Creativity; Doctoral Thesis, Magadh University.

Singh, R.B. Mathur, S.R. And Saxena, S. (1977). Creativity as Related to Intelligence, Achievement and Security-Insecurity. Indian Psychological Review, 14(3), 84-88.

Singh, B. (1986). A Study of Some Possible Contributing Factors to High and Low Achievement in Mathematics of the High School Students of Orissa, Doctoral Thesis, Sambalpur University.

Sinha, S. et al. (1988). A Study of High and Low Achievers With Special Reference to Their Intelligence and Family Variables, *Indian Journal of Clinical Psychology,* 15(2), 103-107.

Sommers, W.S. (1961). The Influence of Selected Teaching Methods on the Development of Creative Thinking. Doctoral Dissertation, University Of Minnesota, Minneapolies.

Spearman, C. (1930). *Creative Mind;* London: Cambridge University Press.

Srivastava, U. and Chandiramani, R. (1995). Scholastic Achievement A Function of Cognitive Style And Family Environment; *Psycho-Lingua,* 25(1&2), 61-64.

Starr, J.W. And Nicholl, C. (1975). Creativity and Achievement in Nuffield Physics; *British Journal of Educational Psychology,* 45, 322-326.

Strenberg, R.J. (Ed.) (1988). *The Nature of Creativity;* Cambridge : Cambridge University Press.

Stein, M.I. (1953). Creativity and Culture, *Journal of Psychology,* 36, 311-322.

Stoddard, G.D. (1943). *The Meaning of Intelligence.* New York: The Macmillan Company.

Stevens, J.C. (1970). A Study Of Creative And Casual

Thinking Skills And Student–Faculty Perception In A Mexican Institution, Ph.D. Thesis; University Of Georgia.

Strauss, J.H. Strauss, M.A. (1968). Family Roles and Sex Differences in Creativity of Children in Bombay and Minneapolis; *Journal of Marriage and Family Life*, 30, 46-53.

Tara, S.N. (1981). Sex Differences in Creativity among Early Adolescents In India; *Perceptual and Motor Skills*, 52, 959-962.

Tardif, T.Z. And Sternberg, R.J. (1988). What Do We Know About Creativity? In R.J. Sternberg (Ed.), *The Nature of Creativity.* Cambridge: Cambridge University Press, 429-439.

Testu, F. (1985). Field Dependence-Independence, Intelligence and Verbal and Non Verbal Performance; *Annual Psychological Abstracts*, 74, 03799.

Taylor, I.A. (1976). Psychological Sources of Creativity; *Journal of Abnormal Behaviour*, 10, 193-202.

Torrance, E.P. (1959). *Explorations In Creative Thinking In The Early School Years. VIII. IQ and Creativity in School Achievement*. Minneapolis, University of Minnesota.

Torrance, E.P. (1962). Cultural Discontinuities and the Development of Originality of Thinking; *Exceptional Children*, 29(1).

Torrance, E.P. (1965). *Rewarding Creative Behaviour;* Englewood Cliffs, NJ : Prentice-Hall.

Torrance, E.P. (1969). *Guiding Creative Talent;* New Delhi : Prentice Hall of India.

Torrance, E.P. (1970). *Encouraging Creativity in Classroom.* Iowa, Dubuque: Win. C. Brown Co.

Torrance, E.P. (1974). *Torrance Tests of Creative Thinking and Manual;* Bensenville : Scholastic Service.

Torrance, E.P. (1984). *Mentor Relationships;* Buffalo, N.Y.: Bearly Limited.

Torrance, E.P. (1987). *The Blazing Drive: The Creative Personality;* Buffalo, N.Y. : Bearly Limited.

Torrance, E.P's *Personal Communication* (1996); Athens, Georgia.

Vandalen, D.B. (1973). *Understanding Educational Research: An Introduction.* New York: McGraw-Hill.

Vernon, P.E. (1938). *The Structure of Human Abilities.* London: Methuen.

Vernon, P.E. (1967). A Cross-Cultural Study of Creativity Tests With 11 Years Old Boys; *New Research In Education,* 1, 135-146.

Vernon, P.E. (1979). *Intelligence: Heredity and Environment;* San Francisco : Freeman.

Vinacke, W.E. (1960). *The Psychology of Thinking.* New York: McGraw-Hill.

Wallach, M.A. and Kagan, N. (1965). Modes of Thinking In Young Children; A Study of The Creativity Intelligence Distinction; New York: Holt, Rinehart and Winston.

Wallas, G. (1926). *The Art of Thought;* New York: Harcourt Brace.

Wertheimes, M. (1959). *Productive Thinking* (2nd Ed.); New York: Harper.

Wechsler, D. (1943). *The Measurement of Adult Intelligence;* Baltimore: The Williams & Wilkins Company.

Witkin, H.A. et al. (1954). *Personality Through Perception.* New York : Harper.

Witkin, H.A. Dyk, R.B., Faterson, H.F., Goodenough, D.R., and Darp, S.A. (1962); *Psychological Differentiation.* New York. John Wiley & Sons.

Witkin, H.A. and Oltman, P.K. (1967). Cognitive Style; *International Journal of Neurophysiology,* 6, 119-137.

Witkin, H.A., Goodenough, D.R. and Karo, S.A. (1967). Stability of Cognitive Style from Childhood to Young Adulthood; *Journal of Personality And Social Psychology,* 7, 291-300.

Witkin, H.A and Goodenough, D.R. (1977); Field Dependence And Interpersonal Behaviour; *Psychological Bulletin,* 84, 661-89.

Witkin, H.A., Moore C.A., Goodenough D.R. and Cox P.A. (1977) Field-Dependent and Field Independent Cognitive Styles and Their Educational Implications; *Review of Educational Research,* 47, 1-64.

Witkin, H. (1978). *Cognitive Styles in Personal and Cultural Adaptation;* Workster, MA : Clark University Press.

Witting, M.A. and Petersen, A.C. (Ed.) (1979). Sex-Related Differences in Cognitive Functioning; *Development Issues.* New York: Academic Press.

Wodtke, K.H. (1963). A Study of The Reliability and Validity of Creative Tests at Elementary School Level; Doctoral Dissertation, University Of Utah.

Yamamoto, K. (1964). The Role of Creative Thinking and Intelligence in High School Achievement; *Psycho. Rep,* 14, 783-789.

Zedeck, S. (1971). Problems with the Use of 'Moderator' Variables; *Psychological Bulletin,* 76, 295-310.